More Effective Programs for a Cleaner Environment

A Statement on National Policy
by the Research and Policy Committee
of the Committee for Economic Development
April 1974

Library of Congress Catalog Card Number: 73-94084
International Standard Book Number:
    Paperbound ($2.00) 0-87186-053-8
    Library binding ($3.50) 0-87186-753-2
First printing: April 1974
Printed in the United States of America by Georgian Press, Inc.
Design: Harry Carter
Photographs: H. Armstrong Roberts

COMMITTEE FOR ECONOMIC DEVELOPMENT
477 Madison Avenue, New York, N.Y. 10022

Contents

Responsibility for CED Statements on National Policy

The Committee for Economic Development is an independent research and educational organization of two hundred business executives and educators. CED is nonprofit, nonpartisan, and nonpolitical. Its purpose is to propose policies that will help to bring about steady economic growth at high employment and reasonably stable prices, increase productivity and living standards, provide greater and more equal opportunity for every citizen, and improve the quality of life for all. A more complete description of the objectives and organization of CED is to be found in the section "CED: A Business-Academic Partnership."

All CED policy recommendations must have the approval of the Research and Policy Committee, a group of sixty trustees whose names are listed on these pages. This Committee is directed under the bylaws to "initiate studies into the principles of business policy and of public policy which will foster the full contribution by industry and commerce to the attainment and maintenance" of the objectives stated above. The bylaws emphasize that "all research is to be thoroughly objective in character, and the approach in each instance is to be from the standpoint of the general welfare and not from that of any special political or economic group." The Committee is aided by a Research Advisory Board of leading social scientists and by a small permanent professional staff.

The Research and Policy Committee offers this statement as an aid to clearer understanding of the steps to be taken in improving the quality of the physical environment for all Americans. The Committee is not attempting to pass judgment on any pending specific legislative proposals; its purpose is to urge careful consideration of the objectives set forth in the statement and of the best means of accomplishing those objectives.

Each statement on national policy is preceded by discussions, meetings, and exchanges of memoranda, often stretching over many months. The research is undertaken by a subcommittee, assisted by advisors chosen for their competence in the field under study. The members and advisors of the Subcommittee on Improving the Quality of the Environment, which prepared this statement, are listed on the following page.

The full Research and Policy Committee participates in the drafting of findings and recommendations. Likewise, the trustees on the drafting subcommittee vote to approve or disapprove a policy statement, and they share with the Research and Policy Committee the privilege of submitting individual comments for publication, as noted on this and the following page and on the appropriate page of the text of the statement.

Except for the members of the Research and Policy Committee and the responsible subcommittee, the recommendations presented herein are not necessarily endorsed by other trustees or by the advisors, contributors, staff members, or others associated with CED.

Purpose
of this Statement

IF THE SOCIAL AND ECONOMIC CONCERNS that inspired this statement about the nation's environmental program were summed up in one sentence, it would be this: Are the most effective and economic ways being used to control pollution and to achieve a high-quality environment in the United States?

Three years ago, when the Research and Policy Committee decided to undertake a study of the environment, the evidence was becoming persuasive that we could not answer this question with confidence. We had come to share with many others in the country doubts that public policies being followed to check environmental deterioration were yielding enough for the money they cost. Too little was being achieved to meet what we perceived to be an urgent need to clean up the environment, a need that remains urgent even as the nation is caught up in an energy problem.

Another consideration also impelled us to make this study. This was the realization that CED had an opportunity to make a unique contribution to the nation's debate over environmental issues. Among CED's trustees, their companies, and their advisors, there were both abundant technical competence and vast experience with federal and other regulatory policies. Systematic use of this intellectual capital could lead to an appraisal of regulatory policies and to recommendations for improvements that might not be obtained in any other way, an assumption we trust is justified by the outcome of our studies.

The costs. An effective program to reduce pollution in this country will be enormously costly for all concerned, not only for business and industry but also for the consumers and the taxpayers who eventually foot the bill. Just how costly it will or should be in dollars and cents cannot be estimated at this time with any precision. There is plenty of room for debate on this point, as demonstrated by comments to be found in the memoranda submitted by the trustees. This is understandable in view of the somewhat unreliable nature of the cost estimates of the present national environmental program and of differences of opinion over just how much such expenditure the nation can afford.

The numbers are important. But before they can be examined meaningfully, there must be a framework within which rational decisions about expenditure can be made.

Vital questions. Unfortunately, in shaping its environmental programs, the nation failed to ask this and related questions involving cost-benefit relationships. Recognizing that the nation wants a high-quality environment, what is the cost at the speed of improvement that is demanded by the public as compared with the cost at some slower speed? What is the cost at various quality levels? What quality levels are really needed or even publicly desired when the facts become known? In other words, what are the trade-offs among various rates of speed and various levels of cost and quality?

Thus, the inexorable economic factors of cost and payment of cost were not balanced against the results actually desired. The public demand for a high-quality environment was brought to bear forcibly but without adequate appreciation of what the costs would be and who would pay them.

Hard-earned lessons. Fifteen years of national experience have now taught several hard-earned and vitally important lessons:

First, a high-quality environment is certainly possible, but an economy that has *no* effects on the environment is not. In short, 100 percent abatement is a sheer impossibility.

Second, it is a mistake to believe that stopping or reversing economic growth will automatically improve the environment. On the contrary, a healthy rate of economic growth is prerequisite for carrying the costs of a rigorous program of environmental protection.

Third, although modest abatement of polluting discharges is possible at low cost in almost all public and private facilities, the incremental costs of abating very high percentages of pollution can be very large indeed.

Because failure to pay proper heed to these essential points will prove increasingly costly for the nation, there is great need for a higher level of economic understanding generally in the nation. Our purpose in this statement is to lay the base for sounder, more effective programs by providing insight into technical and economic limitations of environmental programs and the best ways that resources can be channeled to environmental protection.

The market alternative. We believe that the underlying defect of many of the environmental programs is too heavy reliance on regulation per se as the chief means of controlling the amounts of discharge. This form of control tends to promote excessive governmental interference in the process of decision making and to impose cumbersome, rigid, and often highly uneconomic rules on both public and private dischargers.

Our studies have led us to believe that in many cases a sound and workable alternative to such regulation can be developed. It lies in the use of economic incentives or penalties to encourage businesses and communities to abate discharges. We suggest specific means by which this can be accomplished; for example, effluent fees can be used to curb liquid-waste pollution. The major thrust of our report is to bring environmental considerations within the market framework, insofar as is possible, through what has been called the "polluter-pays principle."

In order to keep our statement within manageable bounds, we have concentrated almost exclusively on the polluting effects of waste materials discharges on the U.S. environment. Beyond the scope of this statement are other important environmental issues such as resource conservation, particularly as it relates to energy problems, and international cooperation in these matters. We hope to deal with aspects of these broad issues in later studies.

Acknowledgments. The Subcommittee on Improving the Quality of the Environment undertook a most difficult assignment in exploring a field of such vast complexity. The extensive research required to carry out this undertaking was made possible by financial assistance from the

Rockefeller Foundation and the Rockefeller Bros. Fund. We deeply appreciate their generosity.

Nor could the subcommittee have hoped to pursue its work without the equally generous sharing of technical expertise by a number of individuals and organizations, to whom we are also greatly indebted.

We would like to acknowledge especially the guidance and leadership provided the subcommittee by its chairman, Robert B. Semple, chairman of BASF Wyandotte Corporation, and the invaluable assistance of the project director, Edwin S. Mills of the Department of Economics at Princeton University.

Two task forces were organized to explore specific environmental sectors. The Task Force on Air Pollution was under the chairmanship of Carroll L. Wilson of the Massachusetts Institute of Technology, who also served as a nontrustee member of the subcommittee. The rapporteur was Michael Massey, Department of Chemical Engineering at Carnegie-Mellon University in Pittsburgh. The Task Force on Liquid Waste was chaired by Fletcher L. Byrom, chairman of Koppers Company, Inc., who was also a trustee member of the subcommittee. The rapporteur was Frederick M. Peterson, Department of Economics, University of Maryland. The members of these task forces are listed on page 74. On behalf of the Committee, we express appreciation for their great help.

Philip M. Klutznick, *Chairman*
Research and Policy Committee

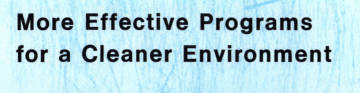

More Effective Programs for a Cleaner Environment

1.

Introduction
and Summary
of Recommendations

‣‣

THROUGH SUCCESSIVE ACTS of legislation by all levels of government over the past decade and a half, the nation has committed itself to bring into being a high-quality environment for all its citizens.* This commitment has profound meaning, both for all those now living and for all those who will follow, because it will determine in great measure the quality of life in this country and will have effects, as well, on the entire world.

We share fully in the conviction that the goal of a high-quality environment should have a high national priority. Pollution lowers the quality of life and, in extreme cases, can affect health and longevity. The air and water environments must not endanger our health and must also be of a quality that will satisfy the rapidly growing demand for outdoor activities and more aesthetic surroundings. Whatever criticisms can be made of U.S. environmental programs (and many faults can be found), the vitally important fact is that this country is now taking major steps toward the goal of improving the environment.

The Council on Environmental Quality estimates that more than $15 billion in public and private funds are now spent annually to upgrade and protect the environment, and it forecasts that by 1981 annual expenditures may rise to $40 billion. The forecast for cumulative environmental expenditures during the decade 1972–1981 is $273 billion, of which about one-third will be public and two-thirds will be private expenditures (see

See Memorandum by *MARVIN BOWER, page 54.

Table 1 and Figure 1). These estimates were made before the fuel short-age intensified in the latter part of 1973 and therefore do not take into account the various cost effects that might result from continued short-ages of some fuels and the changes in standards that might be required. Whatever the costs, they will be borne by the public in the form of higher prices and taxes.

Notwithstanding these costs, we firmly believe that a high-quality environment not only is a legitimate demand but also is one the nation can afford to satisfy. We are convinced by our studies that if certain con-ditions can be met, its attainment is possible within a relatively few years. These conditions involve a proper assessment of costs relative to benefits, the design and effectiveness of programs, and the development of incentives that will maximize the return on the national effort. Properly employed, the nation's resources should be adequate to produce a decent environment without impairing other urgent private and public demands. How to attain this objective is the central concern of this statement.*

EVALUATING COSTS AND BENEFITS

Although modest abatement of polluting discharges is possible at low cost in almost all public and private facilities, the incremental costs of abating a very high percent of pollution can be very large indeed. It is therefore essential that pollution control programs be as efficient as pos-sible and that there be careful evaluation of the benefits and costs of each incremental improvement. As resources are devoted to reducing pollu-tion, those available to satisfy other public and private needs will be re-

Table 1. *It is estimated that annual pollution abatement expenditures in the United States will nearly treble over the decade 1972–1981. The greatest increase is expected to occur in air pollution abatement, resulting from the requirements of the Clean Air Act as amended in 1970. Estimated annual costs of air pollution abatement in 1981 will be about $17 billion, compared with $2 billion in 1972; almost this entire increase in cost will be borne by the private sector.*

See Memorandum by *PHILIP SPORN, page 54.

POLLUTION CONTROL EXPENDITURES, 1971 AND 1981
(billions of 1972 dollars)

	1971			1981		
	O & M Costs a/	Capital Costs b/	Total Costs	O & M Costs a/	Capital Costs b/	Total Costs
AIR POLLUTION						
Public	0.2	0.05	0.2	1.0	0.2	1.2
Private						
Mobile c/	1.1	0.05	1.2	6.2	4.3	10.5
Stationary	0.4	0.3	0.7	4.2	1.5	5.7
TOTAL	1.7	0.3	2.1	11.4	6.0	17.4
WATER POLLUTION						
Public						
Federal	0.2	NA	NA	0.2	NA	NA
State and local	1.2	3.8	5.0	2.6	7.0	9.6
Private						
Manufacturing	0.4	0.3	0.7	2.2	1.5	3.7
Utilities	0.2	0.1	0.3	1.6	0.9	2.5
Feedlots	—	—	—	0.05	0.05	0.05
Construction sediment d/	0.05	NA	NA	0.05	0.05	0.05
TOTAL	2.0	4.2	6.0	6.6	9.4	15.8
RADIATION						
Nuclear powerplants e/	NA	NA	NA	0.05	0.2	0.2
SOLID WASTE						
Public	1.0	0.2	1.2	1.7	0.4	2.1
Private	2.0	0.05	2.0	3.1	0.1	3.2
TOTAL	3.0	0.2	3.2	4.8	0.5	5.3
LAND RECLAMATION f/						
Surface mining	NA	—	NA	0.8	—	0.8
GRAND TOTAL g/	6.7	4.7	11.3	23.6	16.1	39.5

a/ Operating and maintenance.
b/ Interest and depreciation.
c/ Excludes heavy-duty vehicles.
d/ Includes only sediment control for housing and highway construction.
e/ Radiation figures include incremental costs only. The total costs of radiation control are inseparable from other costs of building and operating a nuclear powerplant.
f/ Land reclamation costs are assumed to be current expenditures.
g/ Does not include noise control.

Source: U.S. Council on Environmental Quality, *Environmental Quality: The Fourth Annual Report* (Washington, D.C.: U.S. Government Printing Office, 1973), p. 93.

duced. Moreover, some environmental measures taken to improve the quality of life can prove counterproductive even in terms of this objective if they create serious shortages of energy or vital raw materials. At the same time, it must be recognized that environmental measures may result in direct or indirect economic benefits, for example, by reducing accident rates and improving productivity when severe pollution is reduced.

There is great need for the development of better information about these essential matters and for better public understanding of this information. In particular, it must be recognized that pollution control technology is continuously improving and that abatement programs become uncertain and wastefully expensive if they attempt to go beyond available technology. Moreover, much environmental damage is reversible, and it is important to avoid crash abatement programs that impose excessive instability and costs on the economy.

The energy crisis will have different effects on different sectors of the environmental program. By no means will all the results be negative; in some instances, measures to overcome the energy problem may even accelerate the improvement in environmental quality. For example, scarcities and rising prices of fuels and of various materials will undoubtedly stimulate efforts to develop improved technologies and systems for the recovery and reuse of materials. This should have particular impact on solid-waste disposal systems that create fuel as a by-product, with beneficial results not only in reducing the solid-waste problem but also in lowering air pollution from incinerators.

The shortage and rising prices of fuel should lower air pollution from mobile sources by altering sizes and use patterns of vehicles. An increasing percentage of small versus large automobiles manufactured and sold would reduce pollution. It is to be hoped that technological development will result in auto-emission control devices that will not use more fuel. Higher fuel cost in itself will encourage public transportation and other fuel-saving developments.

At this stage, it is difficult to assess the extent to which such potential benefits will be offset by other factors. Perhaps the major problem caused by the energy crisis will be an increase in air pollution from stationary sources as utilities and other large users of fuel convert to more polluting fuels. Temporary relaxation of standards will undoubtedly have to occur in these areas. On the other hand, such retrenchment will also provide needed time to reconsider and reshape present pollution control programs along the lines recommended in this statement.

DISTRIBUTION OF TOTAL POLLUTION CONTROL EXPENDITURES, 1972-1981

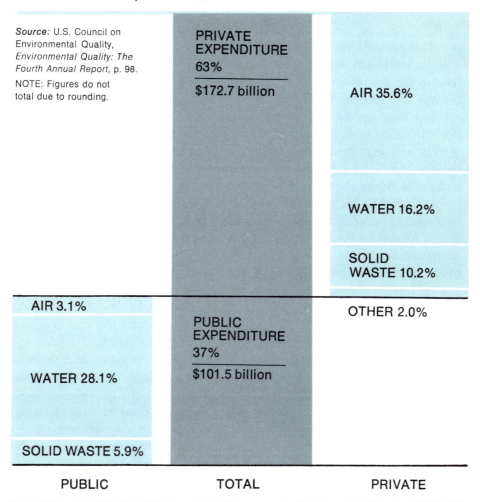

Source: U.S. Council on Environmental Quality, *Environmental Quality: The Fourth Annual Report,* p. 98.

NOTE: Figures do not total due to rounding.

PRIVATE EXPENDITURE 63%

$172.7 billion

AIR 35.6%

WATER 16.2%

SOLID WASTE 10.2%

AIR 3.1%

OTHER 2.0%

PUBLIC EXPENDITURE 37%

$101.5 billion

WATER 28.1%

SOLID WASTE 5.9%

| PUBLIC | TOTAL | PRIVATE |

Figure 1. *Nearly two-thirds of estimated total environmental expenditures during the decade 1972–1981 will be in the private sector.* This compares with a private share of somewhat less than half in 1973. Of an estimated $173 billion in cumulative private spending over the decade, some $150 billion will be over and above what would have been spent by business and industry in the absence of recent federal legislation.

ECONOMIC GROWTH
AND MATERIALS DISCHARGES

It is a mistake to believe that stopping or reversing economic growth will automatically improve the environment. Many of the poorest countries in the world have the worst and most dangerous environments. We believe that continued U.S. economic growth is necessary not only to satisfy unmet public and private needs but also to provide the resources for environmental protection. Increasing emphasis on environmental quality will require changes in the direction of economic growth. Nevertheless, a healthy rate of economic growth is prerequisite to carry the costs of a rigorous program of environmental protection.

Although a high-quality environment is certainly possible, an economy that has no effects on the environment is not. Any economy, regardless of its standard of living, must return to the environment most of the materials it extracts. All returns that exceed the environment's capacity to assimilate them are polluting in the broadest sense. The important decisions facing the nation concern the amounts and kinds of discharge controls it wants to impose, the resources it wants to devote to environmental improvement, and the areas in which resource use can be channeled to environmental protection.

The purpose of economic activity is to produce goods and services that satisfy the needs and wants of the people. Goods production consists of processing materials into forms that are useful to people. Some materials are incorporated directly into consumer products, for example, food, metal in cars, and wood in furniture. But large amounts are used in the production process itself and yet are not incorporated in products. An example is fuel that provides energy to power industrial processes, heat homes, and drive cars.

Materials discharged into the environment often affect people who are remote from the discharge and whose welfare the discharger has neither the ability nor the incentive to consider. Such effects are sometimes called *spillovers*. A homeowner burning leaves or trash has little incentive to take into account the effect of his action on the neighborhood. Until recently, industries and utilities have not generally been required to take into account the effects of discharges on people's health. Local governments usually do not calculate the effects of their sewage on downstream users in another jurisdiction.

To state this point more broadly, markets do not put prices on environmental quality. Raw materials, labor, and other inputs are privately owned and priced. A market economy works well in part because these prices deter wasteful or low-priority uses of valuable productive resources. Because air and most water are in the public domain, markets are unable to put prices on their use. Nevertheless, a high-quality environment is valuable to everybody. It is therefore increasingly necessary, as the population and economy grow, for appropriate levels of government to adopt comprehensive programs that induce people, enterprises, and communities to take account of the effects of their discharges on environmental quality.

REGULATION VERSUS ECONOMIC INCENTIVES OR PENALTIES*

The objective of pollution control programs is clearly to achieve and maintain a high-quality environment. Whatever measures are used to pursue this objective, the ultimate test is some *ambient standard*, that is, the quality of the environment—water, air, and landscape—that surrounds people. The efficiency and cost of any system of pollution control must be measured against this ambient standard.

There are several possible approaches to the problem of discharge control. The most obvious approach, and the one on which the United States has relied, is government regulation of the kinds and amounts of discharges that firms and communities are permitted to make. Essentially, this method identifies sources of undesirable discharges into the air or water and regulates the amount of discharges from such point sources. A first approach to such regulation has been to require a uniform percentage reduction from amounts of discharges in some base period, for example, reducing automobile emissions by 50 percent of the 1970 level.

A major alternative to such regulation is the use of economic incentives or penalties, most prominently effluent fees levied on firms and communities responsible for polluting discharges. The major difference between incentives and regulation is that regulation uses government authority to specify how much discharges must be reduced to reach the desirable ambient standard; whereas economic incentives permit the polluter to rearrange his production or other processes to minimize his cost or maximize his return.

An advantage of regulation is that it is backed by the policing power of governments, which gives certainty to its promises to control dis-

See Memorandum by *ROBERT R. NATHAN, page 55.

charges. Regulation has definitely had the effect of reducing the volume of polluting discharges in the United States. But regulation also has serious disadvantages. It requires extensive intervention by government officials in private activities. It tends to impose cumbersome, rigid, and uneconomic rules on public and private dischargers. It focuses attention and effort on the process rather than on the end result, on technical details rather than on the goal of a satisfactory ambient standard.

Appropriate fees can induce public and private dischargers to abate harmful discharges to the same extent that regulations do, but they permit firms and municipalities flexibility in choosing the means and speed of abatement. Most important, they bring environmental considerations within the market framework by making the polluter pay. This minimizes intrusion of public officials and provides dischargers with continuing incentives to seek further means of abatement. Fees allow the various regions of the country to make appropriate adjustments in order to produce an ambient standard that is generally satisfactory. Finally, their use tends to minimize the distorting effects of environment controls on international competition. The polluter-pays principle has been adopted by the Organization for Economic Cooperation and Development as a means of minimizing such distortions.

We have very carefully considered the merits and disadvantages of these two main approaches and have concluded that the use of fees appears to have the advantage and should be tried to the extent practicable.

It is important to realize that there is no single solution to environmental problems. An approach that works in one area may not work in other areas. Although we favor trying effluent fees where practicable, we recognize that fees should be one among several instruments of environmental policy. Their use should be broadened or narrowed as experience indicates that they are more or less effective than alternative approaches. Whatever policy of discharge control is adopted, it is important that quality goals be justified by specific health and other benefits. Excessively stringent controls waste valuable resources.*

SCOPE OF THIS STATEMENT

In subsequent chapters of this statement, we present a critical review of existing pollution control and solid-waste disposal programs and offer alternative proposals for more effective programs. We are concerned not only with the instruments of environmental protection but also with the

See Memorandum by *HERMAN L. WEISS, page 56.

institutions for planning and administering controls. When it comes to dealing with environmental problems, we have found (as we have also found in our studies of other social problems) that most existing state and local government institutions are poorly organized for an effective attack and that the federal government is too remote from local needs and problems to be able to administer local programs effectively.

This statement does not attempt to deal with all the conditions that affect man's total environment. Restriction of the scope does not imply any judgment of the importance of topics not covered. It has been based on the need to keep our task to manageable proportions. Thus, we have concerned ourselves with the environment only as it is affected by polluting discharges of waste materials and heat. We consider resource conservation only as it is related to issues of pollution abatement. Specifically, one way to reduce polluting discharges is to increase the reuse of materials, which also has a conservation benefit. We leave the broader aspects of conservation, particularly an analysis of the energy crisis, to future studies.

International aspects of environmental problems are only touched on in this report. Some polluting discharges spill over national boundaries and may have global effects on the atmosphere and the oceans. In addition, differences between countries in the character and stringency of environmental controls can have disruptive effects on international trade and can cause hardship and unemployment if products become noncompetitive in international markets. These important and complex issues, which require new forms of international cooperation, are also left for future study.

Serious pollution problems from agriculture, also beyond the scope of this report, will be discussed in a forthcoming policy statement.

Summary of Recommendations

WATER POLLUTION. The most needed reform in the water pollution control program is the creation of effective river-basin authorities and other regional agencies for planning, coordinating, and executing programs for water-quality improvement. Existing institutions do not have sufficiently broad jurisdiction or effective procedures and are often hobbled by overlapping functions and powers. The federal government, which has primary responsibility for pollution control, should delegate that responsibility to river-basin agencies through either federal-state compacts or regional agencies established under the authority of the Environmental Protection Agency (EPA). The federal government would set standads, objectives, and priorities, but each agency would adapt its institutional arrangements and procedures to the changing needs of the region. Bold experimentation with several kinds of river-basin agencies is needed to develop institutions adapted to different regional conditions.

For each river basin or shoreline stretch, we urge that there be single-agency responsibility for planning and executing or controlling all public water-quality programs. The agency should administer discharge control programs in effect in its area and should enforce regulations controlling toxic discharges. It should also have overall supervision of federal grants for construction of waste-treatment facilities in its region. Finally, the agency should be responsible for conducting research and for considering and implementing a wide range of public projects to improve water quality in its basin.*

Market-type incentives offer the most promising alternative to the system of detailed regulations of discharges on which this country has based its national water pollution control program. The best known of these incentives is the effluent fee, which has been used in some European countries. Regional river-basin and shoreline agencies offer an ideal opportunity to experiment with effluent fees as an alternative to existing detailed regulatory programs.

We recommend that the federal government provide for regional experimentation with effluent fees to replace existing regulations and permits as the means of improving water quality. It should offer financial inducements to the regional agencies to experiment with fee systems acceptable to the federal government. The regional agencies should be allowed to use fees collected in their areas for environmental improvement. Fees should be introduced only if they replace existing permit requirements and only after careful evaluation of benefits and costs of alternative ambient water-quality levels. We urge that fees be unchanged for a minimum period of a year and that changes in fees be announced as far in advance as is practicable. Toxic discharges should continue to be carefully regulated.**

AIR POLLUTION. The national program to improve air quality has developed along much the same lines as the program to control water pollution. It is characterized by stringent standards, tough deadlines, ex-

See Memoranda by *E. B. FITZGERALD, by DAVID E. LILIENTHAL, and by FRANKLIN A. LINDSAY, pages 56 and 57.
**EDWARD R. KANE, page 57.

cessive cost, insufficient flexibility, and failure to evaluate costs against benefits. These criticisms apply especially to the program for control of automobile emissions. The standards were set despite the fact the technology was unavailable to produce cars to meet them. Furthermore, given the lead time necessary in designing cars, only a very short period was available in which to undertake a massive research program.

The air pollution control program demonstrates dramatically that: (1) extremely stringent emission standards cause great expense to the public and should be set only after careful calculation of benefits and costs; (2) high standards often require new technology, and therefore lead time should be allowed to permit development of the technology; (3) existing air pollution control programs involve a complex and cumbersome division of responsibility between federal and state governments; and (4) it is important to introduce flexibility in the amount, speed, and means of emissions abatement wherever possible.

We recommend that appropriate environmental agencies carefully consider whether extremely stringent emission standards now existing or envisaged can be justified on the basis of benefit-cost comparisons.*

In the development of agencies with broad authority for handling air-quality control, it should be noted that because air-quality regions do not follow state lines, state governments cannot very well design and implement regional air pollution control programs. What is needed is an agency with jurisdiction over a natural air-quality region, similar to the kind of agency recommended in the development and control of regional water pollution abatement programs. In some regions, it could even be desirable to make a single agency responsible for both air and water programs.

We recommend that a set of natural air-quality regions be designated by the federal government after consultation with state and local officials and that regional air-quality agencies be established to formulate and implement pollution control programs in each region.

In principle, the same arguments that make effluent fees attractive as an alternative to regulation of water pollution hold true with regard to air pollution. But practical problems of implementation are much greater. In the course of our study, it was possible to identify a practical economic incentive for control only in the area of sulfur oxides, where it is relatively easy to measure the sulfur content of fuels. Such a charge would introduce needed flexibility in controlling a major air pollutant, but its adoption would be desirable only if it were used instead of, not in addition to, existing regulations.

See Memoranda by *PHILIP SPORN and by ELVIS J. STAHR, pages 57 and 58.

Although we do not believe that a comprehensive program of effluent fees should be substituted for regulation of air pollution at the present time, we recommend the initiation of experiments that would test the feasibility of substituting economic incentives for the use of regulation aimed at controlling discharges into the atmosphere.*

SOLID WASTE. The problem of disposing of solid waste is susceptible of solution in a reasonably short time if the new technology now being developed is brought into efficient and widespread use through effective organization. Promising improvements are occurring in the techniques of separating materials after collection on a large and economic scale through the use of both mechanical and electrical devices. Reusable materials are recovered, and combustible materials are used as fuel in thermal electric plants. There will undoubtedly be rapid increases in materials reuse in coming years, even though it will not be economic to reuse all or nearly all of many products and even though recycling (reuse for the same purpose) is developing slowly.

Automobiles present a special problem in resource recovery. Several states have recently experimented with fees collected as a part of licensing procedures to provide money for disposal of cars that do not find their way into the recycling system. **We believe that experiments with state fee systems for the disposal of abandoned cars are useful and should be encouraged.**

The use of open dumps as the predominant method of disposing of the country's municipal solid wastes becomes less acceptable each year. **We believe that open dumps must no longer be tolerated in metropolitan areas. We strongly urge that immediate steps be taken by state and local governments in large, settled areas and in many small towns to eliminate all open dumps and to provide sanitary landfills or other alternatives in these areas as soon as is practicable. In small communities, even in outlying areas, where the cost of high-quality disposal methods may not be justified, there should at least be provision for well-operated public dumps.**

In our opinion, the institutional arrangements advocated for water and air are not generally applicable to solid wastes. The appropriate disposal method varies greatly according to type of waste and from community to community. New technology greatly broadens the range of alternatives available to communities; thus, local option and experimentation are desirable.

See Memorandum by *PHILIP SPORN, page 59.

We believe that responsibility for solid-waste collection and disposal should continue to be primarily a state, local, and regional matter and that states should take the lead in establishing appropriate regional agencies for this purpose. We urge continuation of the trend to increased reliance on private enterprise in this sector.

Regional agencies are needed that have broad authority to plan, operate, or contract for a wide range of collection, disposal, and recovery facilities and activities. In this sector, private enterprise and the market mechanism have a particularly effective role to play. The federal government could provide temporary financial assistance through grants from its demonstration program, but continuing federal subsidies are not necessary. State governments should take the lead in the establishment of regional organizations for solid-waste disposal and recovery.* Appropriate regions are usually metropolitan areas. In some cases, interstate, or even international, compacts may be needed.**

See Memoranda by *CHARLES P. BOWEN, Jr., page 59.
**ROBERT C. WEAVER, page 59.

2.

The Economy
and the Environment

ALL MATERIALS EXTRACTED from the environment must eventually be re-turned to it in one way or another (see Table 2). Economic activity changes the form of the materials it processes, but it neither adds to nor subtracts from their mass. Much material is returned to the environment without harming it. But when harm is done, the extent depends very much on the time, form, and place in which materials are discharged. Materials can pollute the environment when they are discharged into the atmosphere, into bodies of water, or to the landscape in ways that impair the usefulness or attractiveness of these environmental components. Al-though massive amounts of materials must be returned to the environ-ment, there are many ways and forms, having very different effects, in which this can be done.

Sewage and other organic material discharged into bodies of water reduce the dissolved oxygen in the water. Lack of oxygen impairs the value of water for fish and other aquatic life and for domestic, industrial, and recreational uses. Many other substances are either toxic or unsightly in bodies of water. Certain gases discharged into the atmosphere are annoying in small concentrations and hazardous to health in large con-centrations.* Trash strewn in dumps or on the landscape is an eyesore and can pollute groundwater and breed vermin. Mining wastes can cause erosion and impair the ecology and natural beauty of the landscape.

16

See Memorandum by *PHILIP SPORN, page 60.

WEIGHT OF BASIC MATERIALS PRODUCED IN THE UNITED STATES, 1965 (millions of tons)

MINERAL FUELS	1,448.0
AGRICULTURE, FISHERIES, FORESTS	607.5
OTHER MINERALS	585.0
TOTAL	2,640.5

Source: Adapted from A. Myrick Freeman et al., *The Economics of Environmental Policy* (New York: John Wiley & Sons, 1973), p. 17.

Table 2. *Materials withdrawn from the environment must eventually be returned to it.* In an affluent, industrialized society, massive amounts of materials are extracted from the environment in the course of economic activity. The estimates in this table include net imports into the United States in 1965. The staggering total of 2.6 billion tons per year comes to about 75 pounds per capita per day, or 13 tons per capita per year, even though the figures exclude large volumes of chemically inactive materials resulting from construction and mining.

The most familiar ways of reducing the impact of materials discharges on the environment are the conventional primary and secondary treatments of domestic sewage before it is discharged. (Primary treatment employs sedimentation or screening; the various methods of secondary treatment include filtering and activated-sludge processes that oxidize the organic matter through the action of microorganisms.) Most industrial wastes can be treated or captured before they are returned to the air or water environment. In addition, alternative industrial processes, generating different kinds and varying amounts of wastes, are available for the production of most goods. Many fuels, combustion processes, and methods of capturing wastes are available to reduce the significant polluting effects of energy conversion. Even domestic refuse can be disposed of in a number of ways, with quite different environmental effects.

But methods of returning materials to the environment vary in cost as well as in environmental effects. Some procedures for the return of materials, as well as certain industrial processes that avoid polluting discharges, are extremely expensive; some clearly are not worth the cost. In addition, some procedures involve great uncertainty because of unproven technology or unknown costs.

Another way to reduce environmental damage from materials discharges is in the forefront of much current discussion: reuse or recycling of materials. Many materials can be used for the same or other purposes once their original uses are finished. Metal from cars and other durable goods can be recycled into metals industries. Glass and paper can be reused. Any organic material can be used for fuel in combustion processes. Materials reuse has both conservation and environmental benefits. It reduces the volume of materials that must be withdrawn from the environment in order to support economic activity, thus conserving natural resources for future use. Correspondingly, it reduces the volume of materials that must be returned to the environment, thus abating pollution.

WATER POLLUTION

Water is of course necessary to sustain life. The water in lakes, streams, estuaries, and oceans also has many industrial, agricultural, recreational, and other uses. Some require that water be withdrawn from its natural watercourse; others make use of the water in its natural setting.* But all uses depend to some extent on the quality of the water. A high-quality public water supply is a primary responsibility of government in all urbanized societies. The United States has long set high standards for public water supply, and as a result, waterborne diseases are much less of a problem here than in many other parts of the world.

Water for drinking and some other purposes, such as various industrial processes, requires very high quality; other uses place only minimal demands on quality. Likewise, there are many ways to measure water quality, and there are different quality classifications for different uses. Natural water bodies serve an important and legitimate function as a means of returning materials to the environment. Through biochemical action, these bodies of water can absorb and degrade limited amounts of materials without loss of quality; even larger amounts can be absorbed

See Memorandum by *PHILIP SPORN, page 60.

INDUSTRIAL AND MUNICIPAL LIQUID-WASTE LOADS
BEFORE TREATMENT, 1968 (millions of tons)

MANUFACTURING	
Chemicals	14,200
Paper	7,800
Food	4,600
Textiles	1,100
Petroleum	550
Primary metals	550
Transportation	160
Machinery	180
All other	530
Total manufacturing	29,670
DOMESTIC (served by sewers)	8,500
TOTAL MANUFACTURING AND DOMESTIC	38,170

Source: U.S. Environmental Protection Agency, Water Quality Office, *Cost of Clean Water,* vol. 2 (Washington, D.C.: U.S. Government Printing Office, 1971), p. 29.

Table 3. *The most important index of water pollution is the biochemical oxygen demand (BOD) that is produced by organic liquid wastes.* These wastes degrade and use dissolved oxygen in the water. It is estimated that industry produced more than three times as much organic waste as the two-thirds of households that are connected to sewers. About 90 percent of organic industrial waste is produced by just three industries: chemicals, paper, and food processing. Agricultural wastes are not included in these data.

without affecting some uses of the water. Excessive discharges of materials, however, impair the ability of water bodies to sustain any use, and can impair the ability of water bodies to regenerate their quality. ———

The best-documented and perhaps the most important index of water quality is dissolved oxygen. Dissolved oxygen determines the kinds of life that can survive in water and affects practically all its uses. When the oxygen content is exhausted, water cannot degrade wastes, and it becomes useless for most purposes. Organic materials discharged to water bodies degrade and use the dissolved oxygen in the process. Thus, the most important single measure of water-polluting activity is the demand made on dissolved oxygen by organic discharges, called *biochemical oxygen demand* or *BOD* (see Table 3).

A second important pollutant is solids such as salts and silts. Salts are corrosive and come mainly from return flow from irrigation. Silts fill up navigational channels and reservoirs, discolor water, and reduce light penetration, thus reducing the water's ability to degrade organic material. Rain carries silt from farms, construction sites, and other land areas and washes it into lakes and streams.

A third pollutant is heat. Heat affects fish life and the ability of streams to cope with organic pollutants and hence also affects the dissolved-oxygen content. Thermal electric plants are the major man-made sources of heat discharges.*

Nutrients, such as phosphates and nitrates, are an increasingly serious source of pollution. They come from organic degradation, whether it takes place in the water body or in a sewage-treatment plant, and from fertilizers that are washed into water bodies from farmland. Nutrients fertilize water, causing the growth of algae, which affects its appearance, taste, oxygen content, and odor.

A large variety of persistent chemicals enter water by discharge from chemical and other plants and inadvertently from such sources as agricultural runoff and acid drainage from mines. Many chemicals are toxic to fish, wildlife, and man, and many cause odors and discolor water.

AIR POLLUTION

Air, like water, is of course necessary to sustain life, and protection of air quality is properly an important responsibility of governments at all levels. In fact, man has fewer options with respect to air than with respect to water. It is possible and even desirable to preserve certain

See Memorandum by *PHILIP SPORN, page 60.

water bodies for swimming and fishing but to permit considerable pollution of others. There is, however, nothing analogous for air; all the air must be fit the breathe wherever people go. Likewise, polluted water can be treated before many uses, but the air must be breathed as it is in its natural state. Thus, the only real option to breathing polluted air is to prevent excessive discharges of materials into the atmosphere.*

The atmosphere, like natural water bodies, can absorb substantial amounts of effluents without undue loss of quality. The discharge of limited amounts of wastes is a legitimate use of both the air and the water environments. Almost no human activity, whether it be breathing itself, heating homes, or moving goods and people, is possible without the discharge of some wastes into the atmosphere. A zero-discharge policy makes even less sense for air than for water.

In practice, economic activity results in the discharge of a great variety of substances to the atmosphere, many of which have at least potentially harmful effects on man, animals, plants, and materials. Many people associate health damage from air pollution with episodes in which pollutants and adverse weather conditions combine to increase sickness and death in a city or metropolitan area for a few days. Such episodes have occurred in the past and may occur again. Most experts now believe, however, that the most serious health effects of air pollution are to cause and to aggravate chronic respiratory and other ailments.

Carbon monoxide, primarily discharged from automobiles, constitutes half of the total pollutants discharged into the air (see Table 4). It is of course a deadly poison in high concentration, but there is no evidence that average urban concentrations are harmful to human health.** High concentrations have been observed in busy parts of large cities under certain conditions, but it is not known whether these amounts have chronic effects on human health. Carbon monoxide levels are negligible outside urban areas and appear to have no adverse effects on vegetation or materials.

Hydrocarbons, also mostly discharged from automobiles, are another major air pollutant. Along with nitrogen oxides, they are agents in the production of photochemical smog, which irritates eyes and the respiratory system and impairs visibility. (Photochemical smog is made up of particles and gases manufactured by the sun mainly out of nitrogen oxides and unburned hydrocarbons.) Hydrocarbons and nitrogen oxides also can damage plants and materials. Although chronic health effects have not yet been clearly demonstrated either from these substances or from smog, continuing research may modify this view.

See Memoranda by *PHILIP SPORN, page 60.
**ELVIS J. STAHR, page 60.

Sulfur oxides result mostly from coal and oil combustion in thermal electric and home-heating plants in and around cities. Many studies have concluded that sulfur oxide concentrations are high enough in metropolitan areas to have measurable effects on mortality and morbidity.[1] Sulfur oxides also damage materials, especially in structures.

Particulates are small particles released into the air by thermal electric plants, home-heating plants, and a variety of industrial processes. They are strongly implicated as causes of adverse health effects where they occur in large concentrations. They also impair visibility and sunlight penetration and damage materials. Fortunately, ambient concentrations have fallen steadily in recent years, mainly as a result of decreased burning of coal in urban areas.

In addition to the materials cited in Table 4, small amounts of many other materials find their way into the air. These include lead and other heavy metals, fluorides, and asbestos. Many of these substances are known to be harmful in high concentrations, and some are possibly harmful at observed concentrations in the urban air. Chronic health effects of low-level exposure to these pollutants are extremely difficult to estimate. Once again, experts are divided with regard to the likely magnitude of such effects, and better information can come only from slow and expensive scientific research presently under way. In the present state of knowledge, it would be perilous to ignore the possibility of chronic health effects, yet it might also be inadvisable to take drastic actions that could prove unjustified in the light of better information.*

SOLID WASTES

The materials listed in Table 5 vary enormously with regard to the potential or actual damage they do to the environment. Much of the agricultural total is plant and animal wastes generated on farms, where they are returned to and enrich the soil without harm to man. But a significant part is animal wastes in feedlots and slaughterhouses, substantial numbers of which are located near population centers, where they can cause serious pollution problems. Most mineral wastes are discharged far from population centers. They are of concern because of massive volumes of solid wastes stored on open ground, because of environmental damage from strip mining, and because of acid drainage from abandoned coal mines.

See Memorandum by *ELVIS J. STAHR, page 61.

MAJOR AIR POLLUTANT EMISSIONS, 1971
(millions of tons)

SOURCE	POLLUTANTS					
	Carbon monoxide	Sulfur oxides	Partic- ulates	Hydro- carbons	Nitrogen oxides	Total
Transportation	77.5	1.0	1.0	14.7	11.2	105.4
Stationary fuel combustion	1.0	26.3	6.5	0.3	10.2	44.3
Industrial processes	11.4	5.1	13.6	5.6	0.2	35.9
Refuse disposal	3.8	0.1	0.7	1.0	0.2	5.8
Miscellaneous	6.5	0.1	5.2	5.0	0.2	17.0
TOTAL	100.2	32.6	27.0	26.6	22.0	208.4

Source: U.S. Council on Environmental Quality, *Environmental Quality: The Fourth Annual Report.*

Table 4. *In the United States, about 1 ton of wastes per person is discharged into the atmosphere in the course of a year.* Carbon monoxide is estimated to be more than half the total pollutants; most is discharged from automobiles, which are also the major source of hydrocarbons, the fourth greatest air pollutant by weight. It should be emphasized that concentrations of pollutants in the atmosphere are not proportionate to discharges occurring over a period of time.

Although residential, commercial, institutional, and industrial wastes account for less than 10 percent of the total, they are a focus of contemporary concern and are therefore so dealt with in this policy statement. The problem is, of course, greatest in urban areas, where disposal sites are increasingly scarce and where poor disposal is a nuisance to millions of people. The 250 million tons per year amounts to about 7 pounds per

SOLID-WASTE GENERATION IN THE UNITED STATES, 1969
(millions of tons)

Agricultural	2,280
Mineral	1,700
Residential, commercial, institutional	250
Industrial	110
TOTAL	4,340

Source: U.S. Council on Environmental Quality, *Environmental Quality: The First Annual Report* (Washington, D.C.: U.S. Government Printing Office, 1970).

Table 5. *Solid wastes in the United States are generated at the estimated rate of some 120 pounds per person per day, or about 21 tons per person a year.* Less than 10 percent of this comes from homes, stores, public buildings, or industrial plants. The overwhelming bulk is produced by agriculture and by the mining industry in extracting materials from the environment. Most agricultural and mining wastes are not removed from the place where they were generated. Because agriculture and mining wastes are included in the above data, the figures in this table are larger than those shown in Table 2.

capita per day and will probably reach 8 pounds by 1980. Municipal wastes (i.e., wastes collected from homes, stores, and factories) account for about 5 pounds per person per day.

Each of the major areas that have been discussed here (air, water, and solid wastes) is explored in detail in the subsequent chapters of this statement, and recommendations are made for appropriate national and local policy to cope with each kind of problem.

3.

Reforming the Water Pollution Control Program

∧∧

THE FEDERAL GOVERNMENT has devoted two decades of effort to the control and abatement of water pollution. Billions of dollars of public and private money have been spent to construct and operate waste-treatment facilities, to make industrial processes less polluting, and to recover wastes before they enter waterways. Many toxic and other harmful discharges have been abated, and the quality of some water bodies is measurably higher (e.g., Lake Washington near Seattle and San Diego harbor). Furthermore, many pollution problems would have become worse had it not been for government pollution control programs.

It is clear, nevertheless, that although there have been some beneficial effects and more may be expected in the future, the benefits have not been commensurate with the cost or effort. Many water bodies near major urban areas are still so polluted that water use is greatly impaired for many purposes. This includes the estuaries of the East Coast cities, the Gulf and Great Lakes ports, and many stretches of the Mississippi system. Indeed, the available evidence suggests that average water quality has deteriorated in the United States since the first national water pollution control act in 1956.[2]

25

NATIONAL WATER POLLUTION CONTROL POLICY

Government regulation of liquid-waste discharges can be said to have started in 1956 with the passage of the Water Pollution Control Act. Under this law, the federal government regulated public and private discharges into interstate waterways. The act specified elaborate and cumbersome procedures: A federal agency had to undertake studies and find that interstate pollution was affecting specific waterways; hearings and conferences with dischargers were required; the government then proposed remedies. After a certain time, the government could sue dischargers for noncompliance in federal court; of course, dischargers could also appeal to the courts. The 1956 act also authorized a matching-grant program for the construction of municipal facilities for waste treatment and a federal research and development program for water pollution control.

The regulatory program set up under the 1956 act was strengthened by subsequent amendments that broadened federal jurisdiction, shortened delays, and made it more difficult for polluters to appeal to the courts.

The 1965 amendments were designed to involve the states in the pollution control program, providing money for states to set quality standards for streams and other bodies of water and to establish schedules for implementing these standards. Violation of the standards would be presumptive of violation of the federal law. In order to encourage the states to set high standards, the amendments required intervention by the federal government to establish standards in those cases where state codes did not receive federal approval.

It was hoped that these measures would increase the enforceability of federal pollution control policies in the courts. However, legal authorities questioned whether standards set under the 1965 amendments were unenforceable in the courts because of the difficulty of relating the failure to meet the standards to the actions of specific dischargers.†

The 1972 amendments, among the most complex ever passed by Congress, constitute by far the most comprehensive changes made in the

---

†In 1970, the federal government started to enforce a provision of the Refuse Act of 1899 that prohibited the discharge of wastes into navigable waterways without a permit issued by the Army Corps of Engineers. Some 40,000 permit applications were received, and the federal government started to grant a few permits, but the issue was made moot by appeal of the requirements to the courts.

Water Pollution Control Act. It sets as goals for industry's pollution abatement activities the use of "best practicable control technology" by 1977, the use of "best available technology economically achievable" by 1983, and the elimination of *all* discharges by 1985. The basic goals of its regulatory provisions are to replace the possibly unenforceable standard-setting procedure of the 1965 amendments, and to avoid the legal challenges to the issuance of permits under the 1899 act. It accomplishes these goals by prohibiting discharges except by permits issued by the states under elaborate supervision and approval of EPA.

Under various amendments to the 1956 act, the provisions of the federal matching-grant program for the construction of waste-treatment facilities have been changed several times. Appropriations have grown over the years, and the matching formula has been changed. Total appropriations grew to well over $100 million per year in the mid-1960s. In 1970, the appropriation was increased from $200 million to $800 million. In 1972, the maximum federal share of the cost of waste-treatment facilities was increased from 55 to 75 percent. In 1973, $5 billion was authorized for such grants, with the amount rising to $7 billion by 1975.

The federal government operates a large research and development program in pollution control technology. Total federal expenditures on environmental research and development, the largest component of which was the liquid-waste program, were about $400 million in 1972. The 1972 amendments authorize a variety of additional sums totaling in excess of $200 million per year.

UNCERTAINTIES
CREATED BY THE 1972 AMENDMENTS

The cumbersome nature of the regulatory provisions of the 1956 water pollution control legislation has been made more burdensome and costly by enforcement policies and procedures. In the earlier years of the legislation, cases were selected arbitrarily, and settlement was protracted. A decade of discussion and negotiation led to unimaginative remedies, with heavy emphasis placed on conventional secondary treatment. They inevitably required uniform percentage abatement of discharges, which is a costly way to achieve improvements in water quality. Changes in processes by which products are made or in the products themselves are sometimes less expensive.

The 1972 legislation can only make the enforcement program more cumbersome and costly. The number of permits that will have to be issued cannot be less than 50,000. Both state and federal governments are required to pass on each application. This places a massive job of central planning in the hands of government. Even an extremely large bureaucracy could not do it effectively without the detailed information on prices, markets, and technology that is available only to knowledgeable operating management. It seems inevitable that the 1972 legislation either will be enforced without vigor or will lead to widespread government regulation of business decisions.

Perhaps most important, the 1972 legislation will introduce great uncertainty into most major investment decisions by business. The legislative guidelines, phased to achieve best practicable control technology by 1977 and best available technology economically achievable by 1983, leave enormous discretion in the hands of public officials. The stated goal of zero discharge by 1985 is undesirable and probably impossible because it implies that no residuals can be returned to the water environment. Businesses will not be able to predict how these provisions will be interpreted and will have no way of knowing in advance whether new or expanded plants will meet legal requirements. It is clear that protracted negotiation with officials and appeals to courts will result.

CREATING EFFECTIVE AGENCIES

Of greatest importance in forming a national water pollution control program is the creation of effective agencies to plan, coordinate, and execute programs for improving water quality. Because water quality is affected by upstream withdrawals, discharges, or other modifications of flow, a river basin forms an integral unit. In the case of lakes, estuaries, and shorelines, the interdependence is even greater because pollutants move in all directions. Yet, many public agencies have responsibility for limited parts of water-quality programs; but typically, no agency has responsibility to ensure that a coordinated plan is developed and followed.

Thus, regulation of discharges is the responsibility of a complex combination of state and federal agencies. Construction of dams and reservoirs to augment streamflow at times of greatest pollution is the responsibility of the Corps of Engineers and the Bureau of Reclamation. Public waste-treatment plants are partially financed by federal and state governments and are planned, built, and operated by local governments. In the case of some potentially important pollution control measures (e.g., in-stream reaeration and transport of water or wastes from one basin to another) no agency is charged with the responsibility.

These present institutional arrangements do not provide sufficiently broad jurisdiction or adequate procedures to achieve goals of improved water quality. There are a variety of river-basin commissions, but most have limited instruments under their control or are limited to planning and advisory functions (see Figure 2). Among existing commissions, the Delaware River Basin Commission comes closest to meeting the need for an agency with broad jurisdiction and powers.

For each river basin or shoreline stretch, we urge that there be single-agency responsibility for planning and executing or controlling all public water-quality programs. The agency should administer discharge control programs in effect in its area and should enforce regulations controlling toxic discharges. It should also have overall supervision of federal grants for construction of waste-treatment facilities in its region. Finally, the agency should be responsible for conducting research and for considering and implementing a wide range of public projects to improve water quality in its basin.*

Because the nation has given primary responsibility for pollution control to the federal government, the federal government would have to delegate its responsibilities to the river-basin agencies. To do otherwise would mean risking continuation of the dual responsibility that has so far plagued pollution control programs in this country. The federal government would have to provide guidelines for the river-basin agencies and ensure that their programs achieve acceptable environmental quality. The federal government could implement this delegation of power by entering into a federal-state compact for a given river basin. Alternatively, it could take direct action and establish a regional agency to carry out regulatory authority conferred by EPA. ——

Final responsibility for decisions on environmental-quality objectives, standards, and priorities would be centered at the federal level. However, each regional agency, whatever its institutional framework, would be free to adapt to changing conditions and to develop procedures and to elaborate concepts in line with the experience and needs of the region. The specific organization and responsibilities should be determined separately for each agency; they need not be the same for each basin. An organization that is ideal for a river basin on the urbanized and industrialized eastern seacoast, for example, might not be adaptable

See Memoranda by *E. B. FITZGERALD, by DAVID E. LILIENTHAL, and by FRANKLIN A. LINDSAY, pages 56 and 57.

to a basin in a predominantly agricultural area of the Midwest. In a large river system, such as the Mississippi, several regional agencies might be required, and representatives of the downstream agencies might participate in the policy-making process of the upstream agencies. Likewise, in some areas, it might be appropriate for some agency members to be appointed and some to be elected.

The important consideration is that a single agency have responsibility and authority to consider and implement a wide range of alternatives regarding water quality and water use throughout a basin and that it be responsible to the affected public. It is also essential that each agency's jurisdiction extend over a significant and coherent basin and that estuaries and shorelines be within the jurisdiction of appropriate agencies.

Bold experimentation with several kinds of river-basin agencies is needed. Only experience with a variety of alternatives will indicate which organizational form is best in specific circumstances. The willingness to change not only institutional arrangements but also jurisdictional boundaries on the basis of experience is essential.

EFFLUENT FEES: ALTERNATIVE TO REGULATION*

Market-type incentives are the most promising alternative to the system of detailed regulations controlling discharges on which this country thus far has based its national water pollution control program. The best-known market-type incentive is the effluent fee, a form of which has been used for decades in the Ruhr Valley in Germany; it has also been used for much shorter periods in some other European countries and has been extensively studied in the United States. The advantages and disadvantages of discharge regulations are well known in this country, but because of lack of experience with effluent fees, the potential advantages of such fees are less well known. (See Appendix, page 63.)

An effluent fee is a monetary charge levied by a government agency on each unit of waste discharged into a body of water (e.g., ten cents per pound of waste discharged). The basic argument for the use of effluent fees is the same as that for the use of market prices in allocating other scarce resources. Prices set in competitive markets allocate resources to high-priority uses and curtail their employment in low-priority uses. The quality of the water in an estuary or a flowing stream is a valuable re-

See Memorandum by *ROBERT R. NATHAN, page 55.

EXISTING RIVER-BASIN AGENCIES

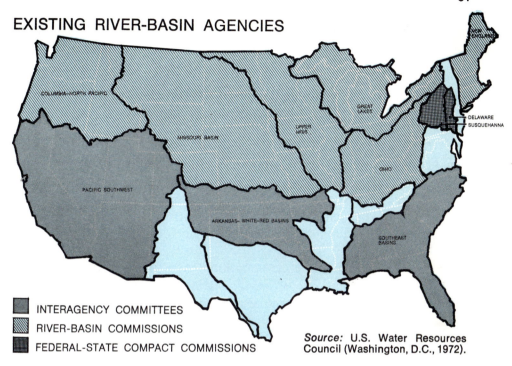

INTERAGENCY COMMITTEES
RIVER-BASIN COMMISSIONS
FEDERAL-STATE COMPACT COMMISSIONS

Source: U.S. Water Resources Council (Washington, D.C., 1972).

Figure 2. *Interagency committees* can be traced back to the natural resources planning bodies established by the government in the 1930s. These committees are composed of federal agencies and departments and have only coordinating and advisory powers. River-basin *commissions,* authorized by the Water Resources Planning Act of 1965, are more comprehensive. State and private interests are represented on the commissions, but their authority is limited to development planning and does not extend to regulation, construction, or management. *Federal-state compact commissions* came into being with congressional approval of the Delaware River Basin Compact in 1961, to which the federal government is a signatory party with the states. The Delaware commission is charged with formulating a comprehensive plan for the development and use of the basin's waters, implementing this broad planning, regulatory, and project-construction powers. A similar compact for the Susquehanna River basin was created in 1970; another embracing the Potomac River is being formed. More limited in purpose but highly effective is the Ohio River Valley Water Sanitation Commission (ORSANCO), organized in 1948 under the first federal water pollution control legislation.

source, but (as noted earlier) competitive markets cannot value it efficiently because it is in the public domain. However, government can set a price for its use for this purpose. Such a price (effluent fee) can limit total discharges into the water body and allocate them proportionally to those for whom discharges are most valuable.

A number of specific potential benefits can result from the use of effluent fees in controlling water pollution.

Effluent fees establish the principle of payment for use of the water environment, which is an important part of the public domain. This is the principle: The water environment is a resource to be used for people's benefit, and one of those benefits is the discharge of waste into bodies of water. But the capacity of water bodies to receive wastes without undue loss of quality is limited, and therefore any discharge into the water should be paid for.

By putting emphasis on results rather than processes, effluent fees place decision making about timing, amounts, and means of abatement in the hands of private firms rather than requiring creation of a duplicate capability at public expense. Under the existing law, EPA is charged with determining best practicable technology for the abatement of pollutants, a determination that must be made individually for each company or plant. It involves such considerations as availability of capital, return on investment, assignment of division or corporate overhead, writing off research and development costs, and depreciation. No agency can determine company policy regarding any of these questions; as a result, best practicable technology becomes an area for extensive disagreement between industry and government agencies. An effluent-fee program should eliminate the time-consuming discussion and determination of what is practicable.

Effluent fees make it possible for society to obtain improvement in water quality more cheaply than is possible with direct regulation of discharges. Regulatory agencies have a tendency to emphasize uniform percentage abatement among all dischargers using a specific basin, particularly through the requirement that all organic wastes receive secondary treatment. But as we noted earlier, this is an expensive way to improve water quality when compared with achieving abatement through changes in processes by which products are made. Effluent fees encourage extensive abatement by those for whom abatement is cheap and modest abatement by those for whom abatement is expensive. A study of the Delaware estuary concluded that modest improvements in water quality might cost only half as much if accomplished by effluent fees as they would if accomplished by uniform abatement of discharges.[3]

Effluent fees provide continuing incentives to dischargers to seek economic means of further abatement. One reason the United States has a highly productive labor force is that high wages provide business with continuing incentives to find ways to economize on labor.* Effluent fees would provide a similar inducement to economize on the use of the water environment. Providing such an incentive is of great importance in the environmental area because of uncertainties about the costs and efficacy of new technology. Permits, on the other hand, provide no incentive to abate discharges that are within amounts covered by the permit.

The likelihood of arbitrary or discriminatory actions on the part of public officials is reduced through a system of effluent fees. Obviously, nobody can guarantee that public policy will not be mistaken, and mistakes can be made with either regulations or effluent fees. When regulations are too stringent or fees are too high, the costs imposed on businesses and communities cannot be justified by benefits from improved water quality. When regulations are lax or fees are too low, water quality will not be sufficiently improved. But effluent fees can be set according to publicly available schedules, and dischargers can be sure that they are being treated equally. Regulatory programs inevitably entail vague guidelines (such as best practicable control technology) that must be interpreted by administrative officials. It is then very difficult to know whether the guideline is applied evenhandedly. It is important, of course, that careful benefit-cost studies of alternative ambient water-quality levels precede the setting of effluent fees. They should be no higher than is necessary to achieve the justifiable water quality.

Finally, a system of effluent fees can help reduce the uncertainty in business and community decision making. Under a regulatory program, there is a danger that guidelines will be interpreted in a different way each year because of changes in elected or appointed officials or in the attitude of the courts. This means businesses can never be sure that, for example, new plants constructed in accordance with current interpretations will be consistent with interpretations at the time the plant becomes operational. The only certainty concerning effluent fees is that they will be changed—a condition that applies to any price or cost. But this can be minimized in the case of effluent fees by a requirement that changes be announced well ahead of the time they become effective.

An alternative economic incentive to an effluent fee is a payment to firms in proportion to their abatement of discharges. Such abatement

See Memorandum by *PHILIP SPORN. page 61.

subsidies have some of the advantages of effluent fees in that they introduce flexibility and continuing incentives into the pollution abatement program. But they have two serious disadvantages in comparison with effluent fees. First, they must be paid for by taxes, and they therefore impose much of the cost of pollution abatement on the general taxpayer rather than on the consumers of goods whose production and use generate the discharges. Second, subsidies are more difficult to administer than effluent fees because they require estimates of the discharges that would have been made in the absence of the subsidy. For these reasons, we believe that abatement or other subsidies are less desirable than effluent fees as a pollution abatement incentive.

FEE SYSTEM WITH SAFEGUARDS

We do not regard effluent fees as a panacea for environmental problems, nor do we overlook the possibilities of abuse that exist in a fee system. Effluent fees are a powerful market force and as such have potential capacity for misuse. But it is likewise true that there is no way to guarantee that any government program will not be misused (witness the abuses that have already occurred in regulatory programs). On balance, it is our judgment that the danger of abuse is less than it is under the existing regulatory system, with its heavy emphasis on permits. We believe that bold experiments with effluent fees should be tried as alternatives to these requirements.

Perhaps the most serious danger is that effluent fees might be imposed in addition to permit requirements. This would prevent fees from performing their basic resource-allocation role, and they would merely burden the present complex regulatory system with a money-raising tax. Thus, we favor the introduction of effluent fees *only* if the existing regulatory system governing the effluents affected is repealed. Discharges of toxic materials should be carefully regulated or in some cases prohibited.

Fees must not be changed unexpectedly; this reduces their value as signals to guide future planning by businesses and communities. Fees may have to be raised periodically as economic growth places greater demands on the assimilative capacity of a body of water. Equally important, it may be necessary to lower fees as quality goals are met. Fees must not be set in capricious fashion nor kept unchanged in the face of new conditions. It is also of vital importance that the views of all interested parties be sought in the fee-setting process. Excessively high fees can result in increased product prices, local unemployment, and industrial dislocation; excessively low fees can result in a poor-quality environment.

It is essential that effluent fees be levied universally on all dischargers (e.g., on discharges from municipal sewers and treatment facilities as well as on those from industrial plants). What is involved here is not merely a matter of transfer of funds from one government agency to another; rather, it is a matter of assuring that all citizens who contribute to water pollution pay their fair share to clean it up. A municipality should have the normal economic incentive to upgrade its waste treatment and reduce its fees, thereby achieving low-cost water-quality improvement in exactly the same manner as industry.*

Finally, it should be pointed out, fees can be levied *only* on point discharges. They are not workable for area discharges such as agricultural runoff. These important sources of pollution must be abated by other means, such as construction of dams to control runoff, development of product controls in manufacturing, and regulation of product use.

We recommend that the federal government provide for regional experimentation with effluent fees to replace existing regulations and permits as the means of improving water quality. It should offer financial inducements to the regional agencies to experiment with fee systems acceptable to the federal government. The regional agencies should be allowed to use fees collected in their areas for environmental improvement. Fees should be introduced only if they replace existing permit requirements and only after careful evaluation of benefits and costs of alternative ambient water-quality levels. We urge that fees be unchanged for a minimum period of a year and that changes in fees be announced as far in advance as is practicable. Toxic discharges should continue to be carefully regulated.

See Memorandum by *CHARLES P. BOWEN, Jr., page 61.

4.

Combating
Air Pollution

THE NATIONAL PROGRAM of air pollution control has developed somewhat more slowly than that of water pollution control, but it is otherwise similar. Federal regulation of air pollutants started with the Clean Air Act of 1963, which authorized the federal government to regulate discharges causing interstate air pollution. Like early provisions for water pollution regulation, it entailed a cumbersome procedure of investigations, findings, and conferences that often led to court cases. There is, however, an important difference: Because there is nothing in air pollution control analogous to municipal waste treatment of water, there is no counterpart to the federal grant program for constructing facilities to treat liquid wastes.

The Clean Air Act has been strengthened by subsequent legislation. The 1965 amendment provided for federal regulation of discharges from automobiles effective with 1968 models. The 1967 amendment considerably broadened the act by empowering a federal agency to publish studies that would identify health and other damages from various air pollutants and describe various techniques of abatement. The states were to use these studies to establish air-quality standards in regions specified by the federal government and to propose plans to meet these standards.

Before the elaborate procedure in the 1967 amendment could be implemented, the 1970 amendment was passed. It gave the states stringent deadlines within which to set and achieve ambient air standards. It also mandated drastic reductions in automobile emissions, amounting to a 90 percent reduction in 1970 levels by 1976, and obligated manufacturers to give five-year or 50,000-mile warranties on emission-control devices on new cars. Finally, this amendment provided for direct federal regulation of emissions from stationary sources constructed after 1970. The amendment did not indicate clearly how direct federal regulation would relate to the ambient standards that the states were enjoined to set and implement.

The final component of federal air pollution control policy comprises research, development, demonstration, and collection data. The federal government first undertook research and data collection specifically for air pollution in 1955, and these programs have been broadened by the Clean Air Act and each of its amendments. In recent years, total federal expenditures for these programs have approached $100 million annually.

EXCESSIVE COSTS AND UNCERTAINTY

Fortunately, data on both pollutant discharges into the air and ambient quality are somewhat better than analogous data for water pollution. Based on these data, there has been some improvement in air quality since the national air pollution abatement program was instituted, and the program must be rated a qualified success.

Between 1940 and 1960, discharges of the major pollutants (listed in Table 4, page 23) increased rapidly, the only exception to this trend being particulate discharges, which remained about constant.[4] But by the late 1960s, total discharges for most pollutants had either leveled off or decreased slightly. Most important, atmospheric concentrations of some of the most harmful pollutants, such as carbon monoxide and sulfur oxides, decreased modestly during the second half of the 1960s. Overall indexes of air quality compiled by the government also show improvement since the late 1960s.

Despite these improvements in air quality, the federal program has been severely criticized. The basic structure of the air program (like that of the water program) has been reorganized several times, changing the relative responsibilities of federal, state, and local governments. The federal government moved slowly, not implementing the original Clean Air Act and its later amendments until 1970; and when implementation finally occurred, little thought was given to the benefits and costs of alternative standards. Very stringent standards had to be met on tight deadlines. Clearly, some standards set under the 1970 amendment cannot be justified by their benefits and costs, and some cannot be met on schedule. The result has been to impose excessive cost, disruption, and uncertainty on business; inevitably, most of these costs will be passed on to the consumer.

Costs escalate rapidly as the requirement for abatement approaches 100 percent, particularly if the abatement must be accomplished so quickly that technology and suppliers of equipment lack time to adjust. For example, stringent controls on emission of one pollutant have in some cases increased discharges of other pollutants. Moreover, there may be other negative effects on the environment because of the methods employed or the energy required to approach the 100 percent level.

Another criticism that the air program shares with the water program is insufficient flexibility. The costs of abatement vary greatly, depending on the details of the process that generates the pollutants, the age of the plant, and the technology available for abatement. Likewise, the benefits of abatement depend not only on the amount to be abated but also on the precise location of the source. Air quality varies greatly between urban and rural locations, among urban areas, and among locations within an urban area. A practical program of air pollution abatement must take into account a variety of local circumstances and must make appropriate use of the atmosphere's assimilative capacity.

An important component of a plan to correct these faults must be an institutional arrangement that permits an abatement program to be designed and executed on a regional basis. Yet almost no progress has been made in designing programs for particular air-quality regions, as mandated under the 1967 amendment, and recent actions have moved in the opposite direction.

PROBLEMS OF THE AUTOMOBILE-EMISSION PROGRAM

Although these criticisms apply to most aspects of the air pollution abatement program, they can be illustrated with special force in the automobile industry. Between 1965 and 1972, auto-emission standards were tightened gradually; 1972 cars emitted only 20 or 30 percent of the carbon monoxide and hydrocarbons emitted by 1967 cars. But the 1970 amendment set extremely stringent standards for 1975 and, especially, for 1976 cars; the latter must emit no more than 10 percent of the carbon monoxide, hydrocarbons, and nitrous oxides emitted by 1970 cars. These standards were set despite the fact that the technology was unavailable to produce cars to meet them, and given the lead time necessary in designing cars, only a very short period was available in which to undertake a massive research program. There was no evidence that the last 5 or 10 percent of abatement would produce benefits that would justify the high costs of achieving those standards.

Equally important, the 1970 amendment contemplated the establishment of annual emission inspections by the states to ensure that cars continued to meet emission standards while on the road. The durability of emission-control devices on the 1975 and 1976 cars apparently will be greater than was thought possible; nevertheless, there is still no guarantee that cars will continue to meet standards for the mandated 50,000-mile period unless owners have them serviced periodically. Furthermore, producers have no way of forcing owners to have their cars serviced. The only way to accomplish this is for states to require annual emission tests, but there has been little progress in implementing that part of the law.

There can be no doubt that the emission-control program has resulted in cars that pollute less than cars available previously. But several lessons, applicable to the entire air pollution control program, can be learned from this experience. First, extremely stringent emission standards are expensive and should be set only after careful calculations of benefits and costs. Second, high standards often require new technology; therefore, it is important to announce such standards far enough in advance to permit development of this technology. Third, existing air pollution control programs involve a complex and cumbersome division of responsibility between federal and state governments. Fourth, it is important to introduce flexibility in the amount, speed, and means of emissions abatement wherever possible.

REGIONAL ARRANGEMENTS AND STANDARDS

The most important reform needed in the air pollution control program is far greater flexibility. There are wide regional variations in quality of ambient air, mix of troublesome pollutants, types of mobile and stationary sources of pollution, availability of technical means of abatement, and costs of achieving particular air-quality levels. Furthermore, as emphasized earlier in this statement, choices are available that determine whether materials are returned to the environment as liquid, gaseous, or solid wastes. All these considerations imply that it is necessary to tailor an environmental program to fit the needs and opportunities of each region.

Because air-quality regions do not follow state lines, state governments are not well qualified to design and implement regional air pollution control programs. What is needed is an agency whose jurisdiction covers a natural air-quality region, similar to the kind of agency we recommend in Chapter 3 for the development and control of regional water pollution abatement programs; we identify several kinds of agencies that could be established for the purpose, noting that the same kind of agency might not be suitable for all regions. The same approach should be applied to programs for air pollution control. It is quite probable that in some regions it will even be desirable to make a single agency responsible for both air and water programs. **We recommend that a set of natural air-quality regions be designated by the federal government after consultation with state and local officials and that regional air-quality agencies be established to formulate and implement pollution control programs in each region.**

Among the activities that should be undertaken by the regional agencies are careful calculations of benefits and costs of alternative air-quality standards. In a period of stringent standards, the incremental costs each time standards are tightened will be very large indeed. Mistaken standards are costly in either direction, but at present, the danger seems to be that standards will be set so high that they cannot be met, cannot be justified, or will be excessively disruptive of the economy. **We recommend that appropriate environmental agencies carefully consider whether extremely stringent emission standards now existing or envisaged can be justified on the basis of benefit-cost comparisons.**

In Chapter 3, we recommend that much greater economy and flexibility can be introduced into the water pollution control program by substituting effluent fees for regulatory provisions of existing laws. In principle, the same arguments make effluent fees attractive as an alternative to the regulation of air pollution. But practical problems of implementation are much greater for air pollutants than for water partly because there is little experience with this form of control.

Only in the area of control of sulfur oxides has a practical economic incentive been studied. It is relatively easy to measure the sulfur content of fuels, and such measurements are now done routinely. Furthermore, if sulfur is not removed from fuels before combustion or from smoke-stacks after combustion, it must be discharged into the atmosphere. Therefore, calculating discharges is not a difficult problem. But technology for continuous measurement of sulfur emissions is unavailable.

In 1971, the President recommended a charge on the sulfur content of fuels. Such a charge would introduce needed flexibility in controlling a major air pollutant. It would, however, be desirable only if it were used instead of, not in addition to, existing regulations.

Although we do not believe that a comprehensive program of effluent fees should be substituted for regulation of air pollution at the present time, we recommend the initiation of experiments that would test the feasibility of substituting economic incentives for the use of regulation aimed at controlling discharges into the atmosphere.

There are many unsolved problems in measuring both discharges and atmospheric concentrations of air pollutants. More research and better instrumentation are badly needed. Meanwhile, flexibility is needed in the means used to measure and control air pollutants. What is best for one pollutant and one air-quality region may not be best under other circumstances.

5.

Solid Wastes:
A Local and
State Responsibility

THE NORMAL MARKET MECHANISMS that work so well in providing consumers with the products they want often do not provide adequate financial incentives to encourage entrepreneurship in the disposal and recovery of *used* products. Local governments have had to take responsibility for solid-waste disposal, which means that disposal costs tend to be paid through local taxes. Consequently, hard-pressed local governments are often unwilling to spend enough money to provide adequate disposal. Furthermore, the fact that local governments may lack appropriate economic incentives and management ability has been an obstacle to the development of recovery systems.

In most communities, the technique of collecting and transporting solid wastes has changed little since the introduction of the compacting truck. Municipal solid-waste disposal consists of five closely related operations: collection, storage, transportation to the disposal site, processing, and disposal. The large compacting trucks that are familiar sights in most cities are the most commonly used collection vehicles. In most areas, the same vehicles that collect wastes are also used to transport them to the disposal site. In some places, however, wastes are loaded onto trains or larger trucks, which may also be used for temporary waste storage at the transfer point, and then transported to the disposal site.

Even more serious and disturbing is the fact that the bulk of municipal solid waste is returned to the environment rather than reused. About 75 percent is disposed of in the cheapest and least desirable way imaginable: open dumps. Another 13 percent goes into sanitary landfills, where each day's wastes are covered with a layer of earth to prevent odors, smoldering fires, eyesores, and vermin; and about 8 percent is burned in incinerators, some with air pollution control devices. About 4 percent of the total is unaccounted for.[5]

These are indeed difficult and large-scale problems. Yet we are confident that they are susceptible of solution in a reasonably short time if the technology that is now developing is brought into effective and widespread use through efficient organization. Some specific suggestions are made in this chapter for creating regional solid-waste agencies. Such agencies would have much greater technical and managerial capability than local governments to plan and operate separation and recovery facilities and to market materials for reuse.

We are also encouraged by the recent emergence of large private companies that collect, recover, and dispose of solid wastes on a large scale and at a profit. Such companies contract for waste removal either with individual households or with local governments. Because competition induces them to employ efficient methods, new technology, and adequate financial resources, they can offer lower costs and improved services in removal, recovery, and disposal. We believe this trend toward the use of private companies to manage municipal solid-waste disposal is desirable and beneficial to all concerned.

Although we know of no simple way to solve the problems of solid-waste disposal through market mechanisms, we are confident that progress must result from experiments with increased reliance on improved managerial methods.

RECOVERY OF
REUSABLE WASTE MATERIALS

Recovery of reusable materials from waste serves three purposes: It lowers pollution by reducing the materials discharged into the environment; it conserves scarce raw materials by decreasing the amounts that need to be extracted from the environment to support a given living standard; and in some cases, it can reduce business costs. But energy expended for recovery must be offset against these benefits.

About 50 percent of municipal waste is paper; 12 percent, garbage; 15 percent, other combustible material; 8 percent, metal; 1 percent, plastics; and 7 percent, glass. The remaining 7 percent is unclassified.[6] This sheer diversity of materials makes the recovery as well as the entire handling of municipal wastes difficult to accomplish because some types of disposal and some methods of recovery require that materials be separated into homogeneous categories. The difficulty has been compounded by the gradual shift in composition from organic materials such as paper and garbage, which will decay or burn, to long-lived synthetic materials such as metals, glass, and plastics.

Fortunately, advances are now being made in this area. Many communities have experimented with requirements that households and other sources of municipal waste separate materials before collection. (Some household solid wastes also are converted to liquid wastes by garbage grinders.) More promising, however, are the improvements occurring in the separation of materials after collection on a large and economic scale through the use of both mechanical and electrical devices. Reusable materials can then be recovered, and combustible materials can be used as fuel in thermal electric plants. This is now being done in Saint Louis and is planned in other cities. Clearly, some innovations are technically feasible, and some can result in substantial cost savings.† There is reason to believe that new technology will be available faster in this area than was thought possible a few years ago.

Meanwhile, technological advances are also occurring in the collection of municipal waste. For example, one community has found it economical to lift trash cans from curbs by a mechanical arm on the collection truck, thus saving labor costs and avoiding injuries to workers. Other experiments have been made with the collection of refuse from dwellings and businesses by vacuum tubes instead of trucks. Such developments could greatly expedite systems of waste recovery and increase their efficiency.

Recovery refers to the separation of materials from the solid-waste stream in order to reuse them. If the purpose of the reuse is the same as that of the original use, the process is often called *recycling*. But in many

---

†Costs of some electrical and mechanical means of separation are about $3 to $5 per ton, or $1 to $2 per household per month.

cases, the best use of recovered materials is a different one from the original use. Recovery can come at the materials-processing stage, at the fabrication stage, or at the end of a product's useful life. In most industries, scrap generated in processing and fabrication is already recovered and recycled back into the industrial process as a normal part of business operations. This is especially true in the metals industries.

Scarcity and rising prices of raw materials have stimulated recovery of industrial scrap in recent years. As raw materials become scarce and their prices rise, it becomes profitable to reuse materials that were previously returned to the environment. In 1972 and 1973, materials prices rose rapidly, and there is evidence that materials reuse accelerated. In addition, fuel shortages dramatically increased interest in the use of mixed organic wastes as fuel in thermal electric plants. It seems likely that the result will be a permanent increase in such materials reuse even if the fuel shortage should lessen in future years. If fuels continue to be in short supply, wastes may become a major supplement to traditional fossil fuels.

Although there will undoubtedly be rapid increases in materials reuse in coming years, it would not be economic to reuse all or nearly all of many products. Economic reuse depends in large measure on the costs of collecting, separating, and transporting used products. The diversity of wastes, the distance to scrap markets, and the costs of processing for reuse will continue to impose limits on materials reuse. However, technical advances can be expected.

Despite growing enthusiasm for recycling, there is little evidence that it has increased the percentage of municipal solid waste reused in recent years. Some municipalities recycle cans and other metal items, but costs of separation and shipment to processors make this uneconomic in many areas. Rubber and plastic are hard to recycle, and negligible amounts are salvaged. Glass is easy to recycle, but the low price of raw materials limits the need to recycle. It has been estimated that about 20 percent of paper products are recycled.

In the main, some stimulus will be given to resource recovery by increasingly stringent air and water pollution control policies. Communities and firms may find it cheaper to recover and reuse materials than to dispose of them in landfills in ways that protect the air and water environments.

Part of the recovery and reuse problem stems from conditions in rail transportation. Scrap or materials for recycling usually have larger volume relative to weight and value than raw materials do. Rail freight rates, which are approved by the Interstate Commerce Commission, make it uneconomic in some cases for railroads to haul products to recycling facilities. Furthermore, many such facilities are set up so that products can be recycled only if they arrive by rail. However, we have not seen persuasive evidence that rail freight rates discriminate against scrap relative to raw materials.* Moreover, we believe that a special subsidy for scrap transportation is undesirable in view of the alternatives available for disposal or reuse.

<h2 style="text-align:center">COLLECTION OF
ABANDONED AUTOMOBILES</h2>

Automobiles not only are the nation's biggest industry but also present one of the biggest solid-waste recovery problems. Because they are not part of the municipal solid-waste system, separate means must be found to facilitate their disposal for recovery and reuse.

About 9 million autos are scrapped each year. The figure increases annually and will soon reach 10 million. Of these, about 15 percent are abandoned by their owners on city streets, fields, and roadsides, where they become eyesores, traffic impediments, targets for vandals, and a major problem for local police. About 85 percent eventually find their way into the hands of specialized dealers. There, usable parts are removed and sold as spares, but the hulks often spend years in unsightly junkyards, awaiting cannibalization and recycling. A variety of technical processes are available for separating, shredding, and compacting autos, and at least some parts of most abandoned cars are eventually recycled into the scrap metal industry.

Recently, rising metals prices have brought most autos to scrap plants after their useful lives are finished. However, the 15 percent of autos that are abandoned mar the landscape in some areas. And a fall in scrap prices, which occurs periodically, means that hulks will again be left in junkyards.

Several states (including California, Illinois, and Maryland) have recently experimented with fees collected as a part of licensing procedures to provide money specifically designated for disposal of cars that do not find their way into the recycling system. The need for such fees may vary from state to state and from time to time. **We believe that experiments with state fee systems for the disposal of abandoned cars are useful and should be encouraged.**

See Memorandum by *ELVIS J. STAHR, page 61.

DISPOSAL SITES

As disposal sites become harder to find, municipal expenditures on solid wastes (currently about $4 billion per year) are bound to rise. Most of this money pays for collection and transportation rather than for disposal or recovery. Collection costs may be somewhat lower in areas of high population density, but transportation costs depend mainly on distances to disposal sites, which are inevitably greater in large cities than in small ones.

The great attraction of open dumps is that they are cheap to operate. Aside from land costs, few communities spend more than fifty cents per ton to dispose of wastes in open dumps. Landfills are inevitably more expensive, although costs vary greatly from place to place and net cost depends on the value of reclaimed land. Aside from land costs and reclamation values, landfill operations usually cost from $1 to $4 per ton of waste. Incinerators require little land, but capital and operating costs may be $5 to $10 per ton, depending partly on what air pollution control devices are used.[7]

Landfills and incineration can provide high-quality disposal if they are sited, designed, and operated properly. An advantage of landfills is that they often increase the value of the land they use; some communities have created parks, golf courses, and other facilities from landfills. Sometimes, however, landfills destroy wetlands that have high ecological value. Incinerators discharge into the air, and solid ash wastes inevitably remain after incineration. Moreover, some materials are not burnable.

The data suggest that methods of disposing of solid wastes are inadequate in many areas. Open dumps are increasingly intolerable in large urban areas. In addition, the volume of solid wastes will inevitably continue to grow in metropolitan areas. Expenditures on solid wastes will undoubtedly grow as higher-quality disposal methods are adopted, and this will continue to be a problem for hard-pressed local governments. But nothing we have seen suggests the solid-waste crisis that some writers have proclaimed imminent. Both the technology and the resources are available to solve the problems; what is needed are the will and the organization to do the job.

The use of open dumps as the predominant method of disposing of the country's municipal solid wastes becomes less acceptable each year. Tipping wastes into a nearby ravine may have been tolerable in an era when waste volumes were modest, the population was small, and most people lived in small towns and rural areas. There was always a place near small communities where the dump would be out of sight and where the odors, smoke, and vermin would annoy few people. But most of today's 210 million Americans live in large, densely settled metropolitan areas. This affluent economy generates enormous volumes of solid wastes, and there are few places to dump them innocuously.

We believe that open dumps must no longer be tolerated in metropolitan areas. We strongly urge that immediate steps be taken by state and local governments in large, settled areas and in many small towns to eliminate all open dumps and to provide sanitary landfills or other alternatives in these areas as soon as is practicable. In small communities, even in outlying areas, where the cost of high-quality disposal methods may not be justified, there should at least be provision for well-operated public dumps.

ROLE OF
LOCAL AND STATE GOVERNMENTS

How is the upgrading of disposal to be brought about? The federal program to persuade communities to close dumps reportedly has led to the shutting-down of 1,000 of the nation's 15,000 dumps. We believe this program should be continued. There is not, however, any evidence that the three-quarters of municipal solid wastes now disposed of in open dumps is much smaller than the total percentage of a few years ago.

Since the 1950s, the federal government has gradually assumed responsibility for water and air pollution control when state and local governments have shown themselves to be inadequate for the task. With the benefit of hindsight, it seems inevitable that the federal government should assume major responsibilities in those areas, as noted elsewhere in this statement. Most important kinds of damage from air and water pollution spill across state and local government boundaries. Although it is tempting to urge that the same pattern be followed with solid wastes and that the federal government gradually assume responsibility for regulating local disposal methods, we believe that it would be unwise to follow this course.

Of course, existing laws empower the federal government to intervene if poor methods of solid-waste disposal result in air or water pollution that has effects beyond the immediate areas. Otherwise, damages from such methods—unsightly dumps, vermin, reduction of neighboring land values, and so forth—are almost entirely local nuisances. These are local problems, and they should be the responsibility of state and local governments.

Furthermore, appropriate disposal methods vary greatly from community to community. In some communities, sanitary landfills are quite adequate; in others, modern incinerators with appropriate air pollution control devices are preferable. And as noted earlier, technology now on the horizon will greatly broaden the range of available alternatives. In this situation, local option and experimentation are desirable. **We believe that responsibility for solid-waste collection and disposal should continue to be primarily a state, local, and regional matter and that states should take the lead in establishing appropriate regional agencies for this purpose. We urge continuation of the trend to increased reliance on private enterprise in this sector.**

REGIONAL AGENCIES

The first need is for state governments to be more aggressive regarding solid-waste disposal in communities within their borders. States are better placed than the federal government to estimate the benefits and costs to their communities of alternative disposal methods. Many states have public health and other laws that require communities to adopt acceptable disposal methods. Likewise, most states have anti-litter laws that prohibit dumping of solid wastes on public streets and parks. But these laws are notoriously unenforced. In many states, the need is simply to enforce laws already on the books. In other states, the laws may be inadequate and need to be strengthened.*

Closing dumps and upgrading disposal facilities inevitably cost money, although the amount varies depending on local conditions, on the amount of resource recovery, and on the disposal method adopted. In some communities, there is a special levy for solid-waste collection and disposal; and in others, private firms contract with households under regulations established by local governments.

In states where local governments are especially hard pressed, it might be appropriate for state governments to share part of the cost of upgrading that they have required of local governments. However, we do not believe there is justification for a federal grant program for upgrading similar to that now in operation for liquid-waste treatment facilities. As we point out in Chapter 3, that program has been too clumsy and wasteful to justify its extension to other areas.

See Memorandum by *FRAZAR B. WILDE, page 61.

To a considerable extent, the solid-waste problem is one of organization rather than one of cost or technology. Almost no local government in a metropolitan area is well placed to have an adequate program of solid-waste collection and disposal. Most such areas are too small to be able to operate a landfill or incinerator of economic size. Many small local governments lack the expertise to be able to compare the benefits and costs of a wide range of alternative disposal and recovery methods, the managerial talent to carry out a plan effectively, and the size to be able to operate modern facilities on an economic scale. In addition, local government jurisdictions are rarely ideal for planning and operating solid-waste collection and disposal. The best locations for landfills and incinerators are mostly beyond the densely settled parts of metropolitan areas, and most local governments in the area lack access to them. Furthermore, the desirable areas in which to have an integrated collection process rarely follow jurisdictional boundaries.

These considerations lead to the suggestion that regional agencies may be desirable for management of solid-waste collection, recovery, and disposal in many areas. Water supply and liquid-waste treatment and disposal have long been handled on this basis in most areas; the case for a similar solid-waste agency seems hardly less compelling. In most areas, the region would be a metropolitan area. The agency might be created by agreement among local governments; better yet, it could be

Figure 3. When the Connecticut Resources Recovery Authority (CRRA) was created in 1973, the state generated an estimated 3.2 million tons of solid waste a year, of which only 5 percent was recovered for reuse. It is anticipated that by 1985 the total will reach some 5 million tons of solid waste annually and that the CRRA statewide system will be processing 85 percent of this and recovering 60 percent. Sufficient fuel will be produced to generate 10 percent of the state's electrical energy and enough ferrous metals, for example, to manufacture 200,000 automobiles. Capital costs of this system are estimated at $295 million, to be financed by tax-exempt bonds. CRRA will operate the system on a self-sustaining basis through the sale of materials and fuels and through user fees ($10 or $12 per ton of solid waste).

CONNECTICUT SOLID-WASTE MANAGEMENT, 1993

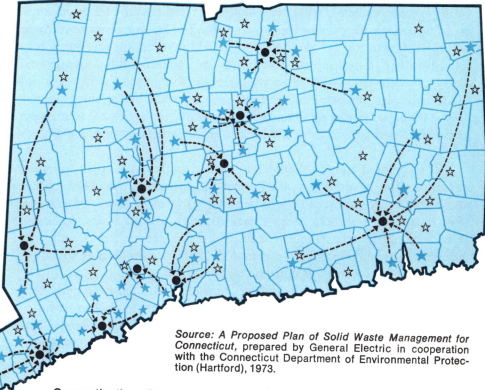

Source: A Proposed Plan of Solid Waste Management for Connecticut, prepared by General Electric in cooperation with the Connecticut Department of Environmental Protection (Hartford), 1973.

Connecticut's solid-waste system will be fully operational in 1993. Its key units will be:

★ 49 local *transfer stations,* which will receive solid waste brought by truck from most of the state's 169 cities and towns

● 10 *resource recovery plants,* located in or near the large urban areas, which will process this waste

☆ 47 *residue sites* and *landfill areas,* located in rural sections of the state, which will receive both residues from the separation process and solid wastes from lightly populated areas

The basic technology used in separation of materials at the resource recovery plants will be the dry-shredding process; there will be experimentation with gas pyrolysis and other technologies for the production of fuel. It is estimated that air pollution from incinerators (10 million pounds in 1973) will be cut in half.

created by the state government or by governments in a metropolitan area. It might also be a private firm. The agency could contract with local governments or directly with citizens for collection and disposal. It could operate vehicles, recovery facilities, and disposal sites itself, or it could contract with private companies to undertake one or more of these activities. Operating at the state level would give an agency the potential advantage of expanding its activities as the metropolitan area grows. Local governments would still have the right to operate their own solid-waste activities and would therefore contract with the regional agency only if it offered better services or lower costs or both. (For a description of the proposed Connecticut solid-waste management system, see Figure 3.)

The regional agency should have broad authority to plan, operate, or contract for a wide range of collection, disposal, and recovery facilities and activities. It should of course be required to meet state and national laws regarding nuisances, health hazards, and air and water pollution. But a regional agency should be well placed to meet such laws, and their enforcement should provide fragmented local governments with incentives to contract for services with the regional agency.

The fact that few such regional agencies now exist suggests that present incentives for their formation are inadequate. Better enforcement of state and federal laws against poor disposal should increase that incentive. So will the desire to take advantage of new technology of waste separation and recycling, which can be applied only on a regional basis. But it is likely that state governments will have to take the lead in establishing regional agencies, in persuading local governments to contract with them, in providing financial inducements to do so, and in some cases, in passing enabling legislation. The federal government could provide temporary financial assistance through grants from its demonstration program, but long-term federal subsidies would not be desirable.*

See Memorandum by *ROBERT C. WEAVER, page 59.

Memoranda
of Comment, Reservation,
or Dissent

Page 3 — by MARVIN BOWER, with which SIDNEY J. WEINBERG, JR., has asked to be associated:

The speed with which this legislation was passed points up the urgent need for a higher level of economic understanding in the electorate. As this policy statement brings out, the public demand for a high-quality environment was made without an adequate appreciation of the costs and who would pay them. Thus, the statement underscores the validity of two economic clichés: "There is no free lunch," and "you can't have your cake and eat it, too."

We must not overlook this opportunity to point up the urgent need under current conditions for a higher level of economic literacy in the nation. This can only be accomplished through economic education. It was for that reason that CED founded the Joint Council on Economic Education in 1949 and for many years contributed financially to its support. (Many supporters of CED are also supporters of the joint council.) The purpose of the joint council is to increase the quantity and improve the quality of economics taught in our schools and colleges. Any reader of this statement who develops a greater recognition of the need for economic education can help to achieve that by urging his school board or school superintendent or college to get in touch with the joint council, a nonpartisan, nonideological organization.

Page 4 — by PHILIP SPORN:

The forecast of a $273 billion expenditure in the decade 1972–1981 is one that needs to give us solid concern. The NASA-Apollo program involved a total expenditure of some $22 billion, but it was stretched out over a period in excess of ten years, or an average expenditure of $2.2 billion per year. The $273 billion projected expenditure on the environment over a ten-year period is 12.5 times as big. Thus, it will involve 12.5 Apollo programs.

The question is not should such an effort be made, but, rather, how wise is such an expenditure, which averages over $27 billion per year. Would it not be a good idea to examine this figure more critically before we so blithely approve its "attainment is possible within a relatively few years" or before we give as our judgment that "properly employed, the nation's resources should be adequate to produce a decent environment without impairing other urgent private and public demands"?

How well can this last assertion be substantiated? Even if we can bring our new productive facilities up to such a standard, can we at the same time correct the abuses of the environment accumulated over many decades, perhaps over as much as a century, and all this "within a relatively few years"? I doubt that any kind of factual analysis will bear this out.

Pages 9 and 30 — by ROBERT R. NATHAN:

In general, I favor as alternatives to direct regulation experimentation with fees that serve as economic incentives or economic penalties. However, this report tends to exaggerate the problems of regulation — and they are big and tough, especially in the context of 1974 Washington — and tends to understate the problems associated with the fee approach.

However it is done, antipollution efforts will entail intervention by government officials in private activities. Fees, to be effective, may require as much intervention as regulation does. Either can be rigid or distorting or uneconomic or unfair. The advantage of use of fees is not so blatantly clear.

The argument that the use of fees is, like the reliance on market prices, a good way of allocating scarce resources has little validity. Presumably, government is to set a price on the volume of polluting discharges. Is that volume the correct measure for setting the fees? What part of the total cost to the polluter of eliminating or reducing discharges does the fee account for? If it is high enough to force some industries to make the capital or operating outlays that are needed to stop their polluting activities, might it not still be low enough to have other plants go on discharging pollutants and pay the fee as the cheapest way to optimize profits? Does a flat rate per unit of discharge hold out prospects of being effective? Will it be fair? Will it take into account how essential a product or service is? Will it give consideration to reasonable time for adjustment?

Yes, experimentation is a very good suggestion, but let us not prejudge the issue. Proper fee approaches may well prove to be the most desirable and effective and equitable and economic alternative. But it may not fulfill all these requirements without necessitating patterns and structures of fees that could be as complex as or worse than direct regulation.

True, regulations are often counterproductive, but has not recent experience revealed that going the price or rate route, when there are no competitive markets, can be costly and harmful. Let us experiment, but that requires an open mind.

Page 10 — by HERMAN L. WEISS:

This policy statement clearly favors the use of a system of effluent fees in preference to a permit system. However, the 1972 amendments to the federal Water Pollution Control Act have already been adopted, and we are thus committed to a national policy of regulatory control of water pollution. In view of the history of government regulations of liquid-waste discharges since 1956 and the legislative history of the 1972 amendments, it does not seem realistic to believe that the newly established permit system would be repealed until it had a fair period of at least several years of testing.

The statement also fails to acknowledge that an effective effluent-fee system would involve administrative challenges and costs that would be at least comparable to those under a permit system. As noted on page 30, effluent fees represent a system of price control and allocation of private use of a resource that is in the public domain. As such, they would entail the same administrative problems faced in any system of price controls and allocations.

Pages 12 and 29 — by E. B. FITZGERALD:

I favor the concept that single regional agencies be responsible for planning and executing or controlling all public water-quality programs. However, I doubt that multiple regional agencies are the appropriate sites for basic research in the field of water quality. Greater technological productivity would more likely result from a single centralized research organization of enhanced professional competence. The role of the regional agencies would then be to apply the output of the central research group innovatively and to provide demonstration facilities to test the validity of concepts developed.

Pages 12 and 29 — by DAVID E. LILIENTHAL; ELVIS J. STAHR has asked to be associated with the second paragraph:

It is unfortunate that this report omits a discussion of the Tennessee Valley Authority. TVA was created as a regional federal corporation, with broad executory authority for the unified development of the several natural resources of a multistate river basin, including of course the resource of the river and its tributaries. The act that established TVA is an instance — the first in our history — of what the report calls "single-agency responsibility."

For reasons of "manageability" (which I can understand), I regret that the report does not so much as refer to the need that a basin agency be concerned with the effect upon water quality of the *totality* of the industrial and agricultural life in the basin and not simply with the input of pollutants. To be effective, the regional agencies surely must see water quality not only as a regulatory preventative function; the problem of water quality extends to the *use* of the streams' water by the people, by the industries, by the farms of a river basin.

Largely because of TVA's overall unified approach to the basin's development, the Tennessee River system is today *cleaner* (i.e., freer of pollutants) than it was forty years ago when TVA began its work, although since 1933 the cities along the river, the industries, and recreational use have multiplied manyfold.

Pages 12 and 29 — by FRANKLIN A. LINDSAY:

I endorse the concept of single-agency responsibility for planning and executing or controlling all public water-quality programs. EPA should be encouraged to try this approach on an experimental basis through selection of an established commission that has the prerequisite powers to carry on a program (such as the Delaware River Basin Compact) and delegation of complete authority to that entity to carry out a water-quality program.

A condition for this delegation must be the willingness of the entity selected to develop new approaches, such as the effluent-fee recommendation that follows.

Page 12 — by EDWARD R. KANE:

The effluent-fee concept is not, in my judgment, an alternative to regulation. Because the fee would be set by federal or regional agencies, it would really be regulation under a different name. Also, a fee system would be considered by many as a license to pollute, which would bring additional criticism to industry and municipalities. For these reasons, I am opposed to the fee concept as it is described throughout this statement.

Page 13 — by PHILIP SPORN:

It has been my observation that EPA is too smug in its conviction of the absolute rightfulness of its rulings and has no patience with those who question its sainthood. Thus, I would recommend the following addition to follow the third line of the recommendation: "and we further recommend that where industry finds itself substantially injured by any unreasonable emission standard, it challenge the reasonableness and legality of the standard in the courts."

Page 13 — by ELVIS J. STAHR:

I agree that the national program to improve air quality has been characterized by stringent standards and tough deadlines — necessarily so, I think. However, I question the flat statement that the national program for cleaner air is also characterized by "excessive cost, insufficient flexibility, and failure to evaluate costs against benefits."

Air pollution inflicts an estimated $16 billion a year in economic damages upon the people of the United States — in the form of illness, lost time, damage to materials, crops, livestock, structures, and so forth. Should consideration be given to how the cost of cleaning up the nation's air compares with the cost of *not* doing so?

Further, the 1970 amendment to the Clean Air Act permits extensions of deadlines. And of course Congress has the power to amend the act (as it was in the process of doing as this comment was written) to provide additional extensions when necessary to cope with specific problems, such as the current energy crunch.

As for the contention that the program fails to evaluate costs against benefits, sight should not be lost of the basic fact that air pollution is primarily a public health problem. Although accurate benefit-cost ratios are very useful, I hope that we will not become obsessed with economic analyses to the point that we hesitate to act expeditiously to protect public health and welfare. A balanced view should include the facts that we are not yet fully applying available pollution control technology, that the cost of doing so has not been a problem for most companies, and that the American public appears to be willing to pay the relatively moderate price increases which have so far resulted from air pollution controls.

Automobile-emission standards were indeed legislated in 1970 before the technology was available to meet those standards. That was a *deliberate* effort by Congress to push industry to speed up its technological development. Has it worked? Consider this point: A Japanese company apparently produced a car in 1973 that met auto-emission standards for 1975 U.S. models. One must at least question the implication that too short a period was made available to U.S. companies for the necessary research and development.

The air pollution control program may well involve "a complex and cumbersome division of responsibility between federal and state governments." I would support proposals to make the program less complex and cumbersome. But I hope we will not lose sight of the need for federal standards and oversight because air pollution is a national problem and must be attacked with at least minimum national controls. States must not be allowed to lure industry from other states at the expense of healthful air.

I support an examination of the justifications for stringent emission standards. Indeed, I believe the National Academy of Sciences is currently studying that very question. I must object, however, to the narrow emphasis on evaluating emission standards solely on the basis of benefit-cost comparisons. The prime purpose of an emission standard must be to control emissions to the degree necessary to protect public health and welfare. The implication that existing or scheduled emission standards are in general too stringent is at least questionable. If a case can be made that specific standards are too stringent, fine; let's make it, but let's cite specifics. The generality casts doubt upon the validity of all standards.

Page 14 — PHILIP SPORN:

This could become a messy sort of affair. It would be very difficult and could lead to absurdities. If a fee system is tried on an experimental basis, it should be for exceeding the ambient air standard at a particular location.

Page 15 — by CHARLES P. BOWEN, JR., with which ELVIS J. STAHR has asked to be associated:

Full consideration and experimentation by means of a demonstration project should be given to the concept of a regulated public utility, with service characteristics and profit levels specified, operating under contract, preferably with the sources of the solid waste.

Pages 15 and 52 — by ROBERT C. WEAVER, with which ELVIS J. STAHR has asked to be associated:

This policy statement affirms that open dumps must no longer be tolerated in metropolitan areas and that state and local governments be strongly urged to take immediate steps to eliminate them as soon as possible. Subsequently, the statement observes that in many states the need is simply to enforce laws already on the books. All this seems to me to be a loose handshake. I don't believe that this report, by exhortation, is going to inspire much action at the state level. If we believe that action has to be taken and soon, I think we have to be more positive.

Although I recognize that this action will depend a great deal upon the states for its achievement, the final sentence still seems inadequate. I feel that the federal government will have to encourage action, which will require financial grants coupled with public education that may or may not have to be continuing. There may have to be sanctions, too.

Page 16 — by PHILIP SPORN:

But many gases are indispensable to life on earth. Carbon dioxide is indispensable to all plant and tree life; sulfur dioxide is indispensable to forest and grain growth.

Page 18 — by PHILIP SPORN:

Still others use water as a transport or diluent medium to make possible the natural breakdown of harmful wastes into harm-free products. From the standpoint of the economy, this is a very important use of water that few industrially developed societies can dispense with.

Page 20 — by PHILIP SPORN:

Even though not man-made, the sun in summertime far exceeds them.

Page 21 — by PHILIP SPORN:

How will this option take care of the 70 million or so in the United States who smoke cigarettes?

Page 21 — by ELVIS J. STAHR:

I disagree with the statement that "there is no evidence that average urban concentrations are harmful to human health." One recalls the story of the tall nonswimmer who drowned in a pond with an *average* depth of three feet. I believe it has been shown that air pollution levels commonly found in some urban areas are indeed harmful to human health. (Moreover, on page 22 the policy statement itself contradicts this statement.)

Page 22 — by ELVIS J. STAHR:

The last sentence in the discussion of air pollution poses one of the dilemmas of pollution control. In attempting to resolve that dilemma, national policy should clearly be to provide an ample margin of safety while awaiting the "better information" that may come along at a later date.

Page 33 — by PHILIP SPORN:

This may be good logic, but I doubt it. One can ask: Has this given the United States the lowest per unit labor cost? And to follow the argument for effluent fees, would it be well to make them just as stiff as the traffic would bear? Just now, we are under the stimulating influence of oil at $17.65 per barrel and steaming coal at $22.00 per ton at the mine. Their beneficent effect on the U.S. economy is not too clearly visible as of February 1974.

Page 35 — by CHARLES P. BOWEN, JR., with which ELVIS J. STAHR has asked to be associated:

It should be emphasized that to be effective, effluent fees must not be regarded as a revenue source. As they have their intended effect and discharges diminish, the resulting revenue reduction should be viewed as a measure of that success.

Page 46 — by ELVIS J. STAHR:

I am still bothered by the statement: "However, we have not seen persuasive evidence that rail freight rates discriminate against scrap relative to raw materials." I have not seen persuasive evidence that they do *not* so discriminate.

Page 49 — by FRAZAR B. WILDE, with which ELVIS J. STAHR has asked to be associated:

As it stands, the program proposed in this section will not be completed in twenty-five years, if ever. If there is to be effective action, states must be directly involved in the direction and the financing of a solid-waste program, which must be set up as a state mandate through the legislature. Such a program should be on a regional basis because many towns will postpone, procrastinate, and fail to participate if enforcement leaves off at mere exhortation.

A state mandate should include some matching grants. If possible, the states should get revenue sharing from the federal government just as they have in terms of sewerage plants and pollution control. The states should establish the regions, help develop the technology, and see that action occurs. Only in this way will we get the advantage of technology based upon large plants using improved methods. Not only will this get the process done; it may even reduce costs through the salvage coming from recycling.

Appendix

The Use
of Effluent Fees
in the United States

INFORMATION REGARDING THE USE OF EFFLUENT FEES in the United States has been gathered and analyzed by an American advisory committee to the Organization for Economic Cooperation and Development (OECD). The report is in the form of answers to questions put by OECD's Business and Industry Advisory Committee (BIAC) to its member groups in twenty-three countries. The purpose of the questionnaire was to elicit information on the experience in these countries with effluent fees and the views of the member groups about the value of such charges as a technique for improving environmental quality.

The group responsible for this report is the Environment Committee of USA/BIAC, which includes representatives of the U.S. Council of the International Chamber of Commerce, the National Association of Manufacturers, and the Chamber of Commerce of the United States of America. The members of this group, together with their affiliations, are listed on page 69.

In some instances, the BIAC report expresses views at variance with the findings of the CED Research and Policy Committee as set forth in this policy statement. It should be emphasized that the opinions expressed in the following report are solely those of the BIAC signatories and do not represent the views of CED's trustees or of any of the advisors or others associated with CED's environmental study. The BIAC report is presented in this appendix for the background information that it provides. A limited amount of editing has been done by the CED staff to make the document consistent with the general style of the policy statement.

Is there any charge system in your country for environmental purposes?

There is no national charge system in the United States, but in a number of municipalities publicly owned facilities charge for treatment of municipal and industrial liquid waste. Four examples are Middlesex County, New Jersey; Minneapolis–Saint Paul, Minnesota; and Greater Chicago and Kankakee, Illinois. Other areas in which experience is available include the Mohawk River basin, Vermont, and Michigan, which has a so-called monitoring fee. An increasing number of private firms contract to remove and treat solid and other wastes for a fee. The federal government is considering some kind of sulfur tax on top of already high standards, with no beneficiation or treatment, and this is generally opposed by business.

What types of charges are levied (i.e., on what products, discharges, and so forth)? Could you give some examples as to the amounts of the specific charges levied?

Charges are generally based on the volume of total flow of liquid waste and on the amounts of pollutants discharged. Generally, only those firms discharging substantial amounts are included in the system, but some systems include households and small businesses on a fixed-fee basis.

The principal discharges on which fees are levied include biochemical oxygen demand; suspended solids; chlorine demand; and fats, oils, and grease. Several systems require firms to control discharge of (1) toxic substances such as mercury or (2) substances that would pass through treatment plants without beneficiation, that would reduce the capacity of the plant to treat other substances, or that would be a public nuisance because of their odor, for example. Kankakee and Minneapolis–Saint

Paul provide extensive listings of these types of substances. Some systems require industries to control discharges themselves at a certain level and treat only the remainder. Some provide financial and even criminal penalties for discharges in excess of ordinance limits; Kankakee offers such an example.

Rates are generally high initially and decline per ton as amounts increase. Some systems charge more for industry outside city limits. Chicago and Los Angeles deduct from the charges levied the amount of sanitation taxes already paid by a firm. In Chicago, charges are computed by the individual firm through the use of measuring equipment and sampling procedures; the authority specifies the frequency of sampling and subjects it to verification.

What is the estimated revenue from pollution charges for the state, region, or any other authority? What is the revenue used for?

Middlesex County revenue in 1971 was over $4 million. . . . Revenues are used to pay off capital costs plus interest on bonds, operating costs of the treatment plant, and sometimes some research.

If liquid waste from an industry is a significant portion of the total (about 30 percent or more of flow and strength), the municipality will usually require a contract with the industry to recover the capital cost of a treatment plant allocated to the industry for the period of financing, regardless of whether the industry is using its allocated capacity or not. An industry may thus acquire a vested interest in a municipal treatment plant during the period of financing. This raises the question of whether a municipality may reassign unused treatment capacity without reimbursement to, or agreement with, the industry to which it was originally allocated and which assisted in the financing of the facility. Another question is whether a municipality may allocate treatment capacity to an existing or new industry that was not anticipated in the original design but was later determined to be available by reason of higher-than-anticipated efficiency because of very conservative design.

The legalities of contracts with a muncipality for capital cost recovery of treatment plant capacity are not well established under the 1972 amendments to the federal Water Pollution Control Act, and it may be several years before well-defined procedures and practices are in use.

There are new regulations in the 1972 amendments that bear on cost allocation to a major industrial user. These require that capital cost of treatment of industrial liquid waste be fully recovered from the industry by a separate identified charge, at least 50 percent of which must be repaid to the federal government in proportion to any federal grants involved.

In your opinion, what is the environmental result derived from the levying of charges?

The Middlesex authority, established in 1950, now treats an average flow of 74 million gallons per day of municipal and industrial liquid waste. Although before-and-after data on the quantity of the receiving stream are not available, it is clear that the quality would be much worse in the absence of this collection and treatment system financed by revenue bonds backed up by a system of charges. In all four cases cited earlier, the intended environmental result is to clean water to an agreed level (standard) by providing treatment to all or that part of liquid waste not treated by the polluter, with the charge sometimes adjusted so that there will be an incentive to provide some treatment at the plant level.

In general, we believe the charge system should relate to the cost of the system of treatment required to achieve a level of quality for an agreed-upon use, such as fishing, swimming, or drinking. At present, such systems are more applicable to water than to air. There might be cases where a legitimate user's charge could be levied without direct treatment being provided, but such cases will be few and are subject to the accusation of being a license to pollute.

In your opinion, what are the advantages or disadvantages of a charge system as compared with a mandatory (regulation) system?

The charge systems described in the above answers are coexistent with a regulation system. The fact that a regulation system exists creates an incentive for industrial companies and municipalities to opt for the system of charges for having liquid waste treated by the regional plant where this is the least-cost solution, as opposed to constructing and operating their own individual treatment plants. This makes the kind of economic sense for which societies should aim. It makes no sense, either from the economic standpoint or from the environmental standpoint, to ponder the advantages or disadvantages of a charge system standing alone as compared with a regulation system standing alone.

We note that using a charge system as described above suggests there is a choice between the amount of payment and control of discharge at the plant level. This implies that the emission-control standard is not set at the highest possible level, which is sometimes the case in the United States. Obviously, charges should not be added in that case because they would serve no environmental purpose. Some industries fear that the attempt to determine what to charge for which pollutant in order to obtain a supposedly desirable standard of water, with a concomitant system of monitoring, collection, and enforcement, is too complicated administratively to be practical. Others note that the alternative of regulation as the only way may also be impractical for attaining the best assessment of cost as compared with benefit for industry and the public. We suggest that any system of charges at present be developed only within local areas where decisions regarding standards, charges, and measures relate to a limited situation and where feedback is relatively easy.

> *Does industry in your country receive any form of economic subsidy for environment purposes from authorities (direct subsidy or taxation advantages of any kind)? If so, what forms do these subsidies take?*

... Generally, no direct subsidies are applicable for capital or operating costs of pollution control in the United States. There is an option available for a five-year write-off of pollution control equipment, and some states accelerate this write-off and also make certain modest exceptions on sales and property taxes. Many states allow tax exemption for interest on industrial revenue bonds for pollution equipment.

Environment Committee of USA/BIAC

Chairman	IAN MacGREGOR (U.S. Council) Chairman and Chief Executive Officer American Metal Climax, Inc.

Vice Chairmen	DANIEL L. GOLDY (U.S. Chamber) President and Director International Systems & Controls Corporation
	EVERETT F. ZURN (N.A.M.) Chairman Zurn Industries

National Association of Manufacturers	DANIEL W. CANNON Director of Environmental Affairs National Association of Manufacturers
	WILBUR W. DODGE Manager, Environmental Control G.O. Caterpillar Tractor Company
	JAMES W. HAUN Vice President and Director of Engineering General Mills, Inc.

Chamber of Commerce of the United States	WINIFRED ARMSTRONG International Economics Department American Metal Climax, Inc.
	JOHN J. COFFEY, JR. Senior Associate Natural Resources and Environmental Quality Chamber of Commerce of the United States
	JOSEPH LING Minnesota Mining & Manufacturing Company 3M Center

U.S. Council of the International Chamber of Commerce	MILES O. COLWELL Vice President, Health and Environment Aluminum Company of America
	F. TAYLOR OSTRANDER Assistant to the Chairman American Metal Climax, Inc.
	RAYMOND W. WINKLER Environmental Conservation Coordinator Exxon Corporation

European Alternate	J. D. MOORE Environmental Coordinator Esso Europe, Inc.

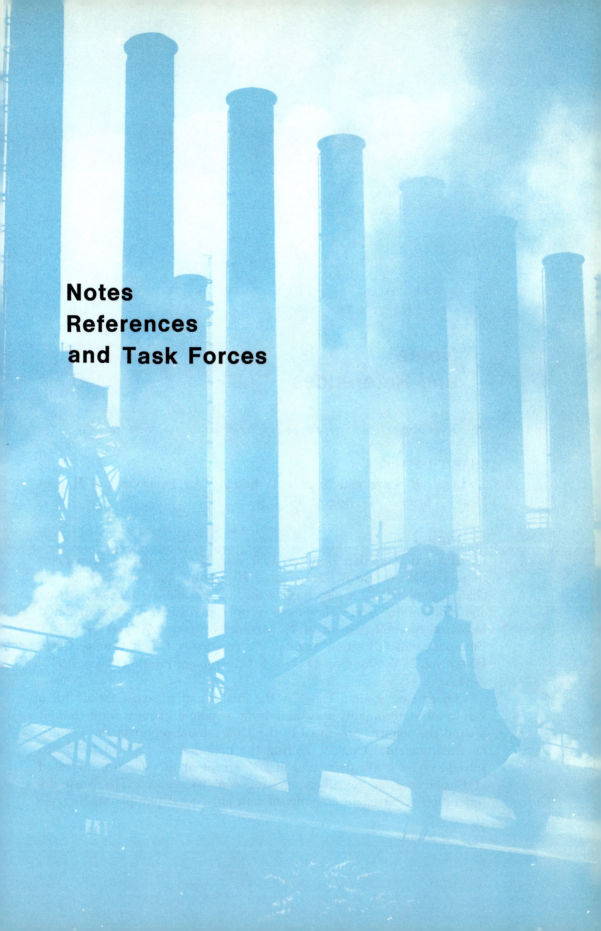

**Notes
References
and Task Forces**

Notes
and References

~~~~~~

CHAPTER 2

1/ Lester B. Lave and Eugene P. Seskin, "Air Pollution and Human Health," *Science*, 21 August 1970, pp. 723–733.

CHAPTER 3

2/ EPA estimates that between 1957 and 1970 discharges from point sources which create BOD increased 10 percent and that nutrient discharges doubled. EPA also reports that of the 260,000 miles of stream and shoreline for which they have records, the waters that are polluted increased from 27 percent to 29 percent between 1970 and 1971. U.S. Environmental Protection Agency, Water Quality Office, *Cost of Clean Water*, vol. 2 (Washington, D.C.: U.S. Government Printing Office, 1971), p. 34.

Of particular significance is the analysis of five-year trends for a variety of water-quality measures from a sample of measuring stations around the country presented in the 1972 annual report of the Council on Environmental Quality. During the period from 1965 to 1970, dissolved-oxygen levels decreased at 20 percent of the stations, increased at 17 percent, and remained unchanged at 63 percent. The worst deterioration occurred in amounts of nutrients; total phosphorus, organic nitrogen, and ammonia increased at 59 percent of the stations and decreased at only 11 percent. Salinity increased at 12 percent of the stations and decreased at 11 percent. Only in the case of suspended solids were there more reports of improvements than of deterioration (30 percent, as compared with 8 percent). The trends reported in urbanized and industrialized areas were worse. U.S. Council on Environmental Quality, *Environmental Quality: The Third Annual Report* (Washington, D.C.: U.S. Government Printing Office, 1972).

3/ Allen V. Kneese and Blair T. Bower, *Managing Water Quality: Economics, Technology, Institutions* (Baltimore: Johns Hopkins University Press, 1968), pp. 158–164.

CHAPTER 4

4/ U.S. Council on Environmental Quality, *Environmental Quality: The Third Annual Report.*

CHAPTER 5

5/ U.S. Council on Environmental Quality, *Environmental Quality: The First Annual Report* (Washington, D.C.: U.S. Government Printing Office, 1970).

6/ *Solid Waste Management,* prepared by ad hoc group for Office of Science and Technology (Washington, D.C.: U.S. Government Printing Office, 1969).

7/ The figures in this paragraph refer to the late 1960s and are taken from the following sources: Arthur J. Warner et al., *Solid Waste Management of Plastics* (Washington, D.C.: Manufacturing Chemists Association, 1970); Jack Demarco et al., *Incinerator Guidelines: 1969* (Washington, D.C.: U.S. Government Printing Office, 1969); Thomas J. Sorg and H. Lanier Hickman, *Sanitary Landfill Facts* (Washington, D.C.: U.S. Government Printing Office, 1970).

Task Force on Air Pollution

Task Force on Liquid Waste

CED: A Business-Academic Partnership

Objectives of the Committee for Economic Development

For three decades, the Committee for Economic Development has had a respected influence on business and public policy. Composed of two hundred leading business executives and educators, CED is devoted to these two objectives:

To develop, through objective research and informed discussion, findings and recommendations for private and public policy which will contribute to preserving and strengthening our free society, achieving steady economic growth at high employment and reasonably stable prices, increasing productivity and living standards, providing greater and more equal opportunity for every citizen, and improving the quality of life for all.

To bring about increasing understanding by present and future leaders in business, government, and education and among concerned citizens of the importance of these objectives and the ways in which they can be achieved.

CED's work is supported strictly by private voluntary contributions from business and industry, foundations, and individuals. It is independent, nonprofit, nonpartisan, and nonpolitical.

The two hundred trustees, who generally are presidents or board chairmen of corporations and presidents of universities, are chosen for their individual capacities rather than as representatives of any particular interests. By working with scholars, they unite business judgment and experience with scholarship in analyzing the issues and developing recommendations to resolve the economic problems that constantly arise in a dynamic and democratic society.

Through this business-academic partnership, CED endeavors to develop policy statements and other research materials that commend themselves as guides to public and business policy; for use as texts in college economics and political science courses and in management training courses; for consideration and discussion by newspaper and magazine editors, columnists, and commentators; and for distribution abroad to promote better understanding of the American economic system.

CED believes that by enabling businessmen to demonstrate constructively their concern for the general welfare, it is helping business to earn and maintain the national and community respect essential to the successful functioning of the free enterprise capitalist system.

Honorary Trustees

Statements on National Policy
Issued by the CED
Research and Policy Committee
(publications in print)

More Effective Programs for a Cleaner Environment *(April 1974)*

The Management and Financing of Colleges *(October 1973)*

Strengthening the World Monetary System *(July 1973)*

Financing the Nation's Housing Needs *(April 1973)*

Building a National Health-Care System *(April 1973)*

*A New Trade Policy Toward Communist Countries *(September 1972)*

High Employment Without Inflation:
  A Positive Program for Economic Stabilization *(July 1972)*

Reducing Crime and Assuring Justice *(June 1972)*

Military Manpower and National Security *(February 1972)*

The United States and the European Community *(November 1971)*

Improving Federal Program Performance *(September 1971)*

Social Responsibilities of Business Corporations *(June 1971)*

Education for the Urban Disadvantaged:
  From Preschool to Employment *(March 1971)*

Further Weapons Against Inflation *(November 1970)*

Making Congress More Effective *(September 1970)*

*Development Assistance to Southeast Asia *(July 1970)*

Training and Jobs for the Urban Poor *(July 1970)*

Improving the Public Welfare System *(April 1970)*

*Statements issued in association with
CED counterpart organizations in foreign countries.*

*Statements issued in association with
CED counterpart organizations in foreign countries.*

*CED Counterpart Organizations
in Foreign Countries

Close relationships exist between the Committee for Economic Development and independent, nonpolitical research organizations in other countries. Such counterpart groups are composed of business executives and scholars and have objectives similar to those of CED, which they pursue by similarly objective methods. CED cooperates with these organizations on research and study projects of common interest to the various countries concerned. This program has resulted in a number of joint policy statements involving such international matters as East-West trade, assistance to the developing countries, and the reduction of nontariff barriers to trade.

CEDA . . . .Committee for Economic Development of Australia

128 Exhibition Street, Melbourne, Victoria, Australia

CEPES . . . .Europäische Vereinigung für
Wirtschaftliche und Soziale Entwicklung

56 Friedrichstrasse, Dusseldorf, West Germany

PEP . . . .Political and Economic Planning

12 Upper Belgrave Street, London, SWIX 8BB, England

経済同友会 . . . .Keizai Doyukai
(Japan Committee for Economic Development)

Japan Industrial Club Bldg.
1 Marunouchi, Chiyoda-ku, Tokyo, Japan

CRC . . . .Centre de Recherches et d'Etudes des Chefs d'Entreprise

31 Avenue Pierre 1ᵉʳ de Serbie, Paris (16ᵉᵐᵉ), France

SNS . . . .Studieförbundet Näringsliv och Samhälle

Sköldungagatan, 2, 11427 Stockholm, Sweden